There are a number of HORIZON CARAVEL BOOKS published each year. Titles now available are:

CHARLEMAGNE
CHARLES DARWIN AND THE ORIGIN OF SPECIES
RUSSIA IN REVOLUTION
DESERT WAR IN NORTH AFRICA
THE BATTLE OF WATERLOO
THE HOLY LAND IN THE TIME OF JESUS
THE SPANISH ARMADA
BUILDING THE SUEZ CANAL
MOUNTAIN CONQUEST
PHARAOHS OF EGYPT
LEONARDO DA VINCI
THE FRENCH REVOLUTION
CORTES AND THE AZTEC CONQUEST
CAESAR
THE UNIVERSE OF GALILEO AND NEWTON
THE VIKINGS
MARCO POLO'S ADVENTURES IN CHINA
SHAKESPEARE'S ENGLAND
CAPTAIN COOK AND THE SOUTH PACIFIC
THE SEARCH FOR EARLY MAN
JOAN OF ARC
EXPLORATION OF AFRICA
NELSON AND THE AGE OF FIGHTING SAIL
ALEXANDER THE GREAT
RUSSIA UNDER THE CZARS
HEROES OF POLAR EXPLORATION
KNIGHTS OF THE CRUSADES

American Heritage also publishes AMERICAN HERITAGE JUNIOR LIBRARY books, a similar series on American history. Titles now available are:

TO THE PACIFIC WITH LEWIS AND CLARK
THEODORE ROOSEVELT, THE STRENUOUS LIFE
GEORGE WASHINGTON AND THE MAKING OF A NATION
CAPTAINS OF INDUSTRY
CARRIER WAR IN THE PACIFIC
JAMESTOWN: FIRST ENGLISH COLONY
AMERICANS IN SPACE
ABRAHAM LINCOLN IN PEACE AND WAR
AIR WAR AGAINST HITLER'S GERMANY
IRONCLADS OF THE CIVIL WAR
THE ERIE CANAL
THE MANY WORLDS OF BENJAMIN FRANKLIN
COMMODORE PERRY IN JAPAN
THE BATTLE OF GETTYSBURG
ANDREW JACKSON, SOLDIER AND STATESMAN
ADVENTURES IN THE WILDERNESS
LEXINGTON, CONCORD AND BUNKER HILL
CLIPPER SHIPS AND CAPTAINS
D-DAY, THE INVASION OF EUROPE
WESTWARD ON THE OREGON TRAIL
THE FRENCH AND INDIAN WARS
GREAT DAYS OF THE CIRCUS
STEAMBOATS ON THE MISSISSIPPI
COWBOYS AND CATTLE COUNTRY
TEXAS AND THE WAR WITH MEXICO
THE PILGRIMS AND PLYMOUTH COLONY
THE CALIFORNIA GOLD RUSH
PIRATES OF THE SPANISH MAIN
TRAPPERS AND MOUNTAIN MEN
MEN OF SCIENCE AND INVENTION
NAVAL BATTLES AND HEROES
THOMAS JEFFERSON AND HIS WORLD
DISCOVERERS OF THE NEW WORLD
RAILROADS IN THE DAYS OF STEAM
INDIANS OF THE PLAINS
THE STORY OF YANKEE WHALING

A HORIZON CARAVEL BOOK

CHARLEMAGNE

By the Editors of
HORIZON MAGAZINE

Author
RICHARD WINSTON

Consultant
HARRY BOBER
Avalon Foundation Professor in the Humanities
Institute of Fine Arts, New York University

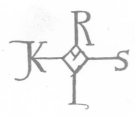

Published by American Heritage Publishing Co., Inc.
Book Trade and Institutional Distribution by
Harper & Row

FIRST EDITION
Library of Congress Catalog Card Number: 68–13721
© 1968 by American Heritage Publishing Co., Inc., 551 Fifth Avenue, New York,
New York 10017. All rights reserved under Berne and Pan-American Copyright Conventions.
Trademark CARAVEL registered United States Patent Office

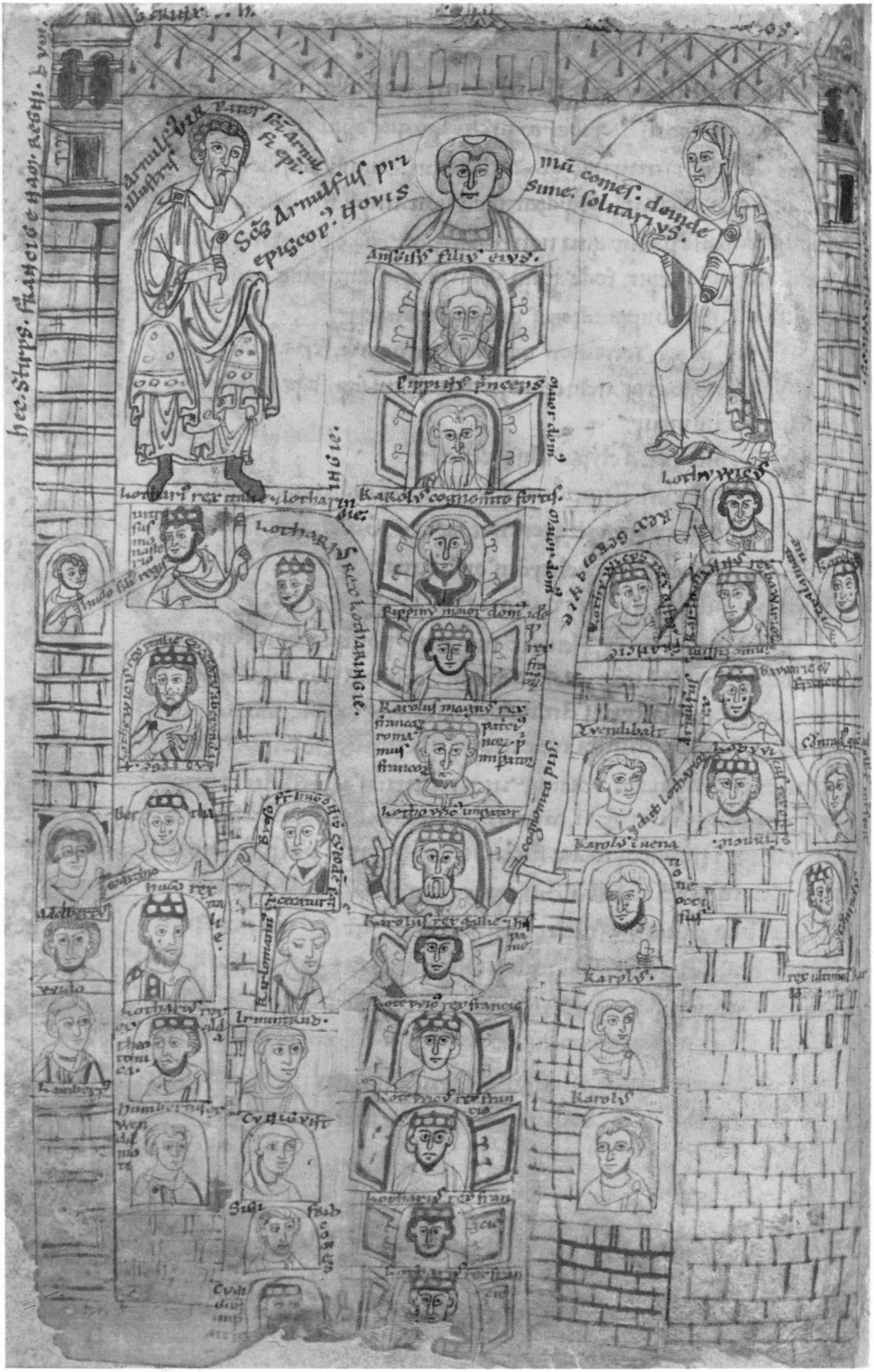

STAATSBIBLIOTHEK, BERLIN; MS. LAT. 295 FOL 80 V

FOREWORD

Even in his own lifetime he was called Charles the Great—Carolus Magnus, Karl der Grosse, Charlemagne, in just some of the languages of people he ruled. In the long sweep of European history, from the decline of the Roman Empire to the flowering of the Renaissance nearly a thousand years later, his is the sole commanding presence. During much of this period, barbarians ranged about Europe, Christianity made only slow progress against paganism, and Western learning was in a state of eclipse. Looking back to these grim times, historians have written of the Dark Ages. Yet, however somber, the period was—momentarily, at least—illuminated by Charlemagne and his brilliant court.

From his father, Pepin the Short, Charles inherited only a part of the Frankish kingdom—little more than half of modern France and the Low Countries. Before his astonishing career was ended, he had conquered half of Europe and his armies had marched through Italy, Germany, and Spain. In a glittering Christmas Day ceremony in Rome, in the year 800, he was crowned the new Roman Emperor.

More than the heroic conqueror of Western Europe, Charlemagne was an intense and thoughtful human being. His succession of five wives brought him a palaceful of children. So warm was his love for his daughters that he could never bear to see them married away from the court, even though enticing alliances with other rulers were offered them. A deeply religious man, Charles became the protector of orthodox Christianity against medieval heresies and argued with monks and bishops about the fine points of Church doctrine. He loved to hunt and built a palace swimming pool in which to develop his aquatic talents. A patron of learning, he established schools and brought artists and scholars to his court to work and study. As a result, most classical literature comes down to us in copies of books made in Charlemagne's time.

Generations of writers and artists turned to Charlemagne's career for inspiration; stylized representations of the great King and Emperor appear in manuscript illuminations made centuries after his death. Numerous examples of these exquisite works, along with statues, artifacts, and jeweled relics, provide rich illustrations to the following biography.

The unity Charlemagne imposed on Europe did not long outlast his lifetime; the title of Holy Roman Emperor he so gloriously inaugurated degenerated into a meaningless label. Nevertheless, the glory of the Carolingian culture he fostered has long outlived his territorial gains.

THE EDITORS

A medieval artist depicted Charlemagne's family tree as descendant royalty peering from castle windows. At top center is the founder, Bishop Arnulf of Metz. Below him appear Pepin (first figure with crown), "Karolus Magnus," and his son Louis, linked to the three sons who shared his realm.

CONTENTS

SONS OF PEPIN

I

In the city of Noyon in northern France, on a crisp October day in the year 768, a great concourse of gaily dressed people assembled in the square before the church. The women wore long dresses with tight sleeves, the wool or linen heavily embroidered. Their blond hair was held in place by circlets set with precious stones—topazes, garnets, and turquoises. The men were clad as colorfully as the women, in knee-length tunics of sea green and blue. Over these they wore long fur mantles that fell almost to their scarlet shoes. Most of them had drooping mustaches and long, flowing hair. And every man carried a sword and a round, leather-covered wooden shield, painted in bright colors or embossed with gold.

Everyone in that throng had fixed his attention on a tall, fair-haired young man with large, flashing eyes who stood beside the ornately robed bishops at the entrance to the church. At a signal from some of the leaders, the whole crowd began to shout: "Hail Charles! May the King live forever!" Then the foremost of the nobles lifted the fair-haired young man on their shields. Raising on the shield was an ancient pagan custom meant to remind the king that he was expected to fight, and if need be, to die for his people—for shields were also used for carrying the dead off the battlefield. But this pagan ceremony was followed by a Christian ritual: the bishops blessed the new King and anointed him with holy oil. The Franks had been good Christians for more than two and a half centuries.

Thus began the reign of the greatest ruler of the Middle Ages. His accomplishments in peace and war would be so remarkable that even during his lifetime "the Great" be-

Raising a king-elect on a shield, the ritual followed at Charles' acclamation at Noyon, is depicted opposite in a tenth-century Byzantine manuscript. Above is a coin dating to Charles' later reign as Roman Emperor.

11

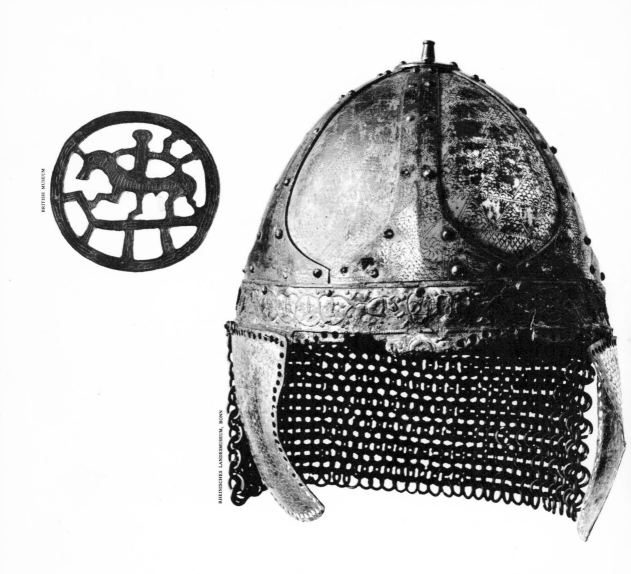

came part of his name. For Charlemagne, as we call him, simply means "Charles the Great" in French. This man was destined to change the history of Europe, and indeed, of the world. But at the time he was elected, crowned, and anointed King of the Franks at Noyon, he was still only an untried youth of twenty-six. What is more, he was not even sole ruler, for that same day another King of the Franks was being crowned in another French city, only some twenty miles away.

By the middle of the eighth century the Franks were a great nation. Three hundred years earlier, they had been only a small group of German tribes living along the estuary of the Rhine River in what is now the Netherlands and in the northern part of Belgium and Germany. But under the rule of a capable and bloodthirsty king named

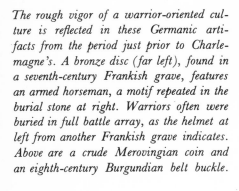

The rough vigor of a warrior-oriented culture is reflected in these Germanic artifacts from the period just prior to Charlemagne's. A bronze disc (far left), found in a seventh-century Frankish grave, features an armed horseman, a motif repeated in the burial stone at right. Warriors often were buried in full battle array, as the helmet at left from another Frankish grave indicates. Above are a crude Merovingian coin and an eighth-century Burgundian belt buckle.

Hludowig or Clovis—the name is really the same as our modern Louis—they had conquered much of western Germany and the Roman province of Gaul.

In the fifth century the Roman Empire was breaking up. Hard-fighting, land-hungry Germans from many different tribes swept into the helpless seats of Roman civilization and set up petty kingdoms. But Clovis and his successors, the kings of the Merovingian dynasty, began the slow process of reuniting some fragments of the empire. Clovis had been converted to Christianity under the influence of his Christian wife; and with his reign there began that special close relationship with the Christian Church that was to set the Franks apart from their neighbors.

The Merovingian descendants of Clovis allowed the actual power of government to slip from their hands. The kings let their major-domos, the chief stewards of their households, do all the work. Soon the "mayor of the palace," as the Latin *major domus* is traditionally rendered, was actually giving orders to his masters. After a while, says Einhard, Charlemagne's friend and biographer, "there was nothing left for the king to do but to be content with his name of king. . . . He had nothing that he could call his own beyond this vain title of king, and the precarious support allowed by the mayor of the palace." The Merovingians had become "do-nothing kings." As members of a ruling family do, the mayors of the palace passed on their office from father to son, but they always kept a figurehead Merovingian on the throne. The Franks considered their kings sacred, and the mayors of the palace did not quite dare to rule in their own name.

The dove of the Holy Spirit, according to legend, descended with holy oil for the baptism of Clovis in 496. Bishops (left) and nobles, one holding the Frankish crown, attend the immersed King at his historic conversion.

By the middle of the eighth century, however, Pepin the Short, Charlemagne's father, decided that he could risk doing without the puppet king. But how was he to acquire that sacred character that the people considered an essential part of kingship? Pepin reasoned that only approval from the highest religious authority in the Christian world would make his usurpation of the throne acceptable to the people.

Pepin therefore sent Abbot Fulrad of St. Denis to Rome with a message for the Pope. Fulrad was a great statesman as well as abbot of St. Denis, the great monastery—just outside of Paris—where the kings of Frankland were buried. The abbot had a hand in all the business of government and was in fact a kind of unofficial prime minister. He also came to serve as tutor of Pepin's two sons, Charles and Carloman.

An unflattering portrait of Childeric I (above), Clovis' father, appeared on the gold signet ring found in his tomb. Below, Pepin the Short, who deposed his Merovingian descendants, is depicted on a bas-relief in a German church.

Abbot Fulrad told the Pope that Childeric III, the present King of the Franks, was feeble-minded and so could not rule. What was to be done about him? Hard pressed by enemies in Italy, the Pope was counting on help from the Franks. Diplomatically he answered that "it is better to give the name of king to him who has the wisdom and the power, rather than to him who has only the name of king without the authority."

The Pope's words meant the end of the Merovingian do-nothing kings. When Fulrad returned from Rome with his historic message, Pepin the Short had Childeric's head shaved—removing the long hair that symbolized his royalty—and sent the deposed King to a monastery to spend the rest of his days as a monk. According to the religious feeling of the times, once a man "renounced the world"—willingly or unwillingly—and became a monk, he could never again return to his previous life or position. It was widely believed that those who tried to come back to "the world" —and some did try—were sure to suffer divine punishment. Pepin could thus consider Childeric safely out of the way.

Germanic tribes had long followed a custom of electing or acclaiming their rulers, and in 751 Pepin persuaded the Frankish nobles to elect him King of the Franks. He was crowned by his friend Bishop Boniface, the "Apostle of the Germans"—the great missionary from England who had devoted his life to converting the many still-pagan tribes among the northern and eastern Germans. At the coronation of Pepin, Boniface introduced a rite practiced in his homeland by the Anglo-Saxons: he consecrated Pepin by

15

Born in England around 680, Boniface was sent by Pope Gregory II to Germany, where his success in organizing Christian churches led to his consecration as a bishop in 723. Three years after the coronation of Pepin, Boniface resigned as Archbishop of Mainz and left on a missionary journey to Frisia, where a martyr's death awaited him (right). A volume he was carrying at the time of death (above) still bears the marks of sword cuts.

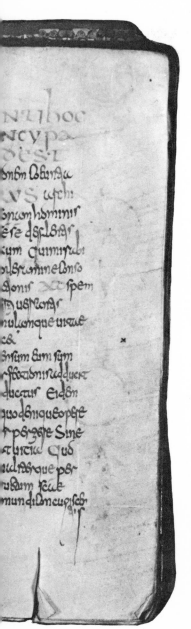

anointing him with holy oil. Boniface probably also suggested the second novelty at this ceremony: for the first time in the history of the Franks the queen—Pepin's wife, Bertrada, or Berta—was also crowned and anointed.

The two sons of Pepin and Bertrada may have been present at the coronation. Charles was then nine—he was born in 742, perhaps on April 2—and his brother, Carloman, was several years younger. And that, strangely enough, is all that can legitimately be said about the first eleven years of Charlemagne's life. His early years are shrouded in mystery; contemporary records are silent.

One can only guess about Charles' education from what is known of his later life. He certainly learned to read and write, for he became a considerable scholar. The widely held notion that he could not write is based on a misinterpretation of a passage in Einhard's biography of him—the only biography we have by someone who knew him personally. Einhard relates that as a grown man Charles used to keep a slate and copybook under his pillow, so that he could practice his hand in shaping letters. "He did not get far because he had begun too late in life," says Einhard.

Einhard was not referring to ordinary writing but to calligraphy—the fine script in which manuscripts were copied. This "Carolingian minuscule" was a beautiful new handwriting, and the printed letters used today are based on it. The monks made calligraphy a fine art—and that was what Charles could never learn. He could certainly scribble well enough for workaday purposes. He also dictated a good deal, just as busy statesmen do today.

N en po trencer del nou nul blane.
Dist braibant el uos uamale mane.
Se non a ores macon et truigane.
E ne carui en nostra uite un bestant.
Maquando tu uo p̄uuer bon conuiant.
Se tu no reuoie damenete esant.
Plu te conar or cuit et argant.
Tant non oie inquia uesti pomne.
L asez ester balasino ebelisant.
Wi lier uos conaro plu bela tra tant.
Dist .k. lep̄iser uos semant.
No la p̄ua laser ueno lo p̄tenant.
Por moi amor p̄eso oie baregamant.
Dist braibant eo teu faro do liant.
Wom conuen adnienz oda libiant.
Comenz braibant ferir de la spee·
Sanz lon gaual·
A m sin sire ta neuos co la uoi.

N os cristian tel usanca tenon.
Dapue cont pris muler cote beneicion.
Mais en saine tant cu muo son.
Par nul autre cancer nela p̄ion.
Dist le pain un par los cu bricon.
Tu morras eloeli sant aueron.
Au rois galasino la p̄ise nos isauon.
Dist .k. aico beneicion.
Pois qe ce sen crap̄ase delte mon.
De le no aueio blasmo ne rep̄ienson.
Mes an cor no si ne mento u abatu daigon.
Dist le pain tosto uos cō quiron.
T en duien tarda al intreo son.
Feri leuue mais elrio su bricon.
S uant se stra corne dan anci ala u agon.
Si qe braibant nole co se que seno de tre la igon.
Uos mire oie fate de lauserat guason.
El caileto fe cau ali sablon.

At home Charles spoke German. He also mastered the vulgar Latin—rapidly becoming French—that was spoken by the people in the more Romanized parts of his father's kingdom. He knew the formal Latin that was used in all writing; and he had some knowledge of Greek, although he understood it better than he spoke it. A school for the sons of nobles was part of Pepin the Short's court, and Charles went to that, in addition to taking private lessons from Abbot Fulrad. In his boyhood Charles learned at least enough of grammar, logic, rhetoric, arithmetic, music, astronomy, and geometry to hold his own among the "thinkers" and "grammarians" he invited to his own court in later years. Charles had an active, questing mind; nothing could be further from the truth than the picture sometimes found in histories and biographies of a rough, uncultivated man who achieved what he did by sheer forcefulness.

Not that Charles lacked force. He was renowned for his strength, his courage on the battlefield, his skill and endurance in hunting and swimming. Riding was as natural as breathing to him, for his father's court never stayed long in one place. The king and queen and all their attendants were on the move constantly, traveling from palace to palace, as the royal manor houses were called by courtesy. In reality most of these palaces were just big farms. The king's wealth consisted of these farms; there was no efficient system of taxation in the Frankish kingdom. It was easier for the king and his followers to use up the produce of the royal estates by moving to each place in turn than it was to have oxcart-loads of provisions and goods brought many miles over bad roads.

Communications were slow and clumsy in Frankland; centuries of neglect had reduced the great Roman roads to muddy tracks. There was another reason for "the royal progress," as the king's journeys were called. Only by going about the country could a ruler administer justice and make sure that his lower officials did not abuse their authority. But it was a trying life, especially for children. Perhaps Charles suffered a good deal from the discomforts of travel during his boyhood and for that reason, among others—including, of course, the need for rapid movement

Around Charles' reputation for valor later artists created legends, especially about the unknown years of his youth. The imaginative illustrations opposite show his combat initiation: Unhorsed by an opponent (top), he rallies to strike a mortal blow (below, left) and claim his victim's helmet.

19

The difficulties of travel in medieval times were shared by king and peasant alike, as the details above and right from an eleventh-century manuscript show. The monarch's horse-drawn, two-wheeled chariot was no doubt swifter but certainly little more comfortable than the farmer's larger oxcart.

of his troops—took a lifelong interest in the state of the roads throughout his realm.

At the age of eleven Charles at last makes his appearance in the contemporary records. The annals—brief chronicles of each year's events that were kept by the monks in various parts of the kingdom—mention under the year 753 that young Charles was sent to greet Pope Stephen II on his arrival in Frankland and conduct him to his father. The Pope's visit to Frankland must have been tremendously exciting to everyone, and especially to the son of parents as deeply religious as Pepin and Bertrada were. This was the first time any pope had ever stepped on Frankish soil. And Charles' own awe swelled when his father led a great retinue of Frankish nobles out on the highroad to salute His Holiness. Pepin bowed to the ground before the Pope and then took the bridle of his horse as if he were a groom and walked ahead of the Supreme Pontiff toward the royal palace at Ponthion.

In the summer of 754 Pope Stephen himself repeated the coronation of Pepin and Bertrada. This time Charles and his brother also felt the drops of holy oil touch their heads. Young as they were, they were proclaimed kings of the Franks along with their father. The Pope also gave Pepin and his sons the titles of Patricians of the Romans. That was a vague honor that meant whatever the holders wished it to mean. Pope Stephen hoped that the "three Kings of the Franks," as he called them thereafter, would feel obliged to protect Rome and the papacy.

The Pope had come all the way from Rome to ask Pepin for help against the Lombards, who were then pushing

deeper and deeper into Italy. The Lombards were a Germanic tribe who had once been neighbors of the Franks in northern Germany. During the great wandering of the nations from the fourth to the sixth century, the Franks had moved only a short distance westward, but the Lombards had crossed the whole of Europe from north to south. Streaming into Italy, the Lombards set up a kingdom of their own, in that part of northern Italy that ever since has been called Lombardy. They also founded two big duchies in the central and southern parts of the Italian boot. Squeezed in between these two Lombard powers was a narrow strip of land that legally belonged to the Eastern Roman Empire.

The Roman emperors at Constantinople appointed governors for this territory in central Italy. The governors were called exarchs, and since they made the fortress-city of Ravenna their capital, the whole territory was known as the Exarchate of Ravenna. It included Rome, which meant that the popes were subjects of the Roman emperor at Constantinople. As long as the emperor defended his subjects, the popes did not mind this arrangement. But the empire, though still very strong, could not supply enough troops for every outpost. Ravenna was far from Constantinople and did not seem very important. In 751, the same year that Pepin was crowned King of the Franks, the Lombard King, Aistulf, at last succeeded in capturing formerly impregnable Ravenna. He then demanded that Rome herself submit to him.

For nearly two hundred years the popes had fended off the Lombards by diplomacy and by playing on their religious authority. And since the time of Pope Gregory the Great (590–604), they had been virtually the rulers of Rome. But King Aistulf refused to be awed, even when the Pope spoke as if he were St. Peter in person. Aistulf savagely swore that he would cut off the heads of all the Romans with a single sword unless they submitted to him. That was the desperate situation when Pope Stephen II undertook his long journey to Frankland. Unless Pepin would help, he said, Rome was lost.

Pepin, who owed his crown to the papacy, believed it was his Christian duty to aid the Holy Father. Shortly after his second coronation in 754, Pepin—ignoring the objections of his nobles, who did not want to campaign far from home—led an army across the Alps into Italy. The Lombards met this army in the mountains; but they had little heart for fighting the ferocious Franks: Pepin's small ad-

Carloman's signature appears on a 769 document confirming a land grant to an abbey in his kingdom.

A thirteenth-century inventory of the Rhineland Abbey of Prüm contains this picture of Charlemagne (right), appropriately towering over his father, Pepin the Short. Above in heaven, God blesses the abbey's two principal benefactors.

vance guard defeated the whole Lombard host (Pope Stephen called it a miracle); and King Aistulf barely escaped capture by sliding undignifiedly down a rocky slope. The Frankish army marched on unopposed to the gates of Pavia, the capital of Lombardy. By then Aistulf was ready to give up. Suing for peace, he offered a large sum of money in tribute.

Pepin granted easy terms, and as a result, had to repeat his campaign two years later in 756. After the second expedition he gave to the Pope the lands of the Exarchate of Ravenna—twenty-three cities and castles in all. This famous Donation of Pepin, added to the Duchy of Rome, created the Papal States. In a way the Donation still exists, for the tiny area of Vatican City at Rome remains an independent papal state.

Young Charles probably rode with his father on the first campaign into Lombardy, when he was only twelve. He certainly did so on the second, for by fourteen a boy was almost old enough to fight. From Pepin's two wars with the Lombards the future Charlemagne learned some military strategy. But above all he probably learned that it was easier to win a war than to keep the gains. That lesson was forcibly impressed on him during the last years of his father's life. Much of this time Charles spent fighting in Pepin's army in the Duchy of Aquitaine.

Aquitaine, in what is now southwestern France, was a

23

Reverential yet proud, a kneeling Pepin presents his famous Donation to Pope Stephen II, enthroned in his Roman palace. Holding aloft the papal tiara he helped preserve for the Pope, Frankland's King points to five walled cities rising in the hills of Italy— part of his award to the Pontiff. Pepin's seizure of the Exarchate of Ravenna from the Lombards and his subsequent presentation of the conquered territory to the Pope was the basis for the thousand-year-long reign of Stephen's successors over much of central Italy. The 1350 miniature painting at right commemorated the six hundredth anniversary of Pepin's historic gift.

Semi-independent for two and one-half centuries after its initial conquest by the Franks, the duchy of Aquitaine maintained its own royalty until subjugated by Pepin in 768. The battered crown above, belonging to an eighth-century ruler of Aquitaine, bears fleurs-de-lis, the iris symbol used in later centuries by French royalty.

land of great cities and a rich commercial life, as well as a fruitful country of vineyards and sheep farms. At this time it extended all the way from the Loire River to the Pyrenees and from the Allier River to the Atlantic Ocean. Waves of invaders—Vandals and Visigoths, Saracens and Franks—had passed over Aquitaine. Nevertheless, Roman speech and the Roman arts of living had survived there longer than in many parts of Italy. Roman baths, aqueducts, and amphitheaters were still in use; and something of the old Roman military spirit had lingered on also. Year after year, under their heroic Duke Waifar, the Aquitanians rose in rebellion against the Franks, their nominal overlords. Summer after summer, with Charles now taking active command of troops, King Pepin marched into Aquitaine, seizing castles, storming towns, ravaging the countryside, burning villages and vineyards. He repeatedly defeated the Aquitanians in the open field, but Duke Waifar always evaded him, went into hiding, and returned to the fray as soon as the Frankish army withdrew. Waifar was always able to recruit fresh troops, because the Aquitanians were defending their homes against a foreign enemy.

At last Pepin accomplished his ends by treachery. He bribed or otherwise persuaded some of Waifar's attendants to assassinate their master. With the death of Duke Waifar, the Aquitanian war seemingly ended for good.

Pepin did not long outlive his foe. At the end of the summer's campaign in 768 he fell ill with a fever. Although he offered prayers at the tomb of St. Martin in Tours, he did not mend. His sons and grieving wife carried him to Paris, where, on September 24, he died, after dividing his kingdom more or less equally between Charles and Carloman. Such division had been the ancient practice of the Merovingian kings and of their mayors of the palace also. It had led to many wars between brothers in the past; but Pepin trusted to the strong character of his wife, Queen Bertrada, to keep peace between their sons.

The two young kings buried their father with great pomp in the Abbey of St. Denis. Then each went to the capital of his half of the kingdom—Carloman to Soissons, and Charles to Noyon. Each summoned his nobles to an assembly to confirm Pepin's will; for the kingship was still, in theory, elective. The Franks had prospered under Pepin the Short, and they unhesitatingly took oaths of loyalty to his sons. On Sunday, October 18, both Charles and Carloman were crowned Kings of the Franks, each in his own capital city.

Bishops dominate this version of Charles' coronation as King of the Franks from the Grandes Chroniques de France, *a manuscript dating to about 1375. The artist, attempting to link the great medieval emperor to the kings then ruling France, embroidered Charlemagne's robe with fleurs-de-lis.*

II

A KINGDOM UNITED

Throughout the history of the Franks there had been a great deal of bad blood among royal brothers over the question of inheritance. The division of the kingdom between Charles and Carloman predictably aroused ill feeling, and within a few months of their dual coronation, the brothers quarreled. Pepin had given half of Aquitaine to each so that both would have an interest in controlling that troubled duchy. But when the indomitable Aquitanians rose in revolt once more, in the summer of 769, Carloman refused to aid his brother in suppressing the rebellion. Charles marched alone, with what forces he had, and easily won the first of the many military victories that were to give him a reputation for invincibility. Within two months he completely pacified Aquitaine, as his father had never succeeded in doing; and thereafter the duchy remained a loyal part of the Frankish kingdom.

The bitterness between the brothers lingered. Indeed, it might have led to war if Queen Mother Bertrada had not intervened. In those early years of both reigns she wielded great influence and contrived to maintain a precarious peace between her two sons.

Bertrada also made efforts to reduce the tensions between the Frankish and the Lombard kingdoms. She arranged a marriage between Charles and a Lombard princess, the daughter of King Desiderius, who had succeeded King Aistulf. Charles already had a Frankish wife named Himiltrude; but there were good grounds for divorce. There was some question about the legality of Charles' marriage to Himiltrude, a commoner; and she had borne

In the tenth-century drawing at left Charlemagne appears as a middle-aged monarch with a drooping mustache. His crown and scepter bear fleurs-de-lis but the copyist has forgotten the orb his open right hand must have held in the original version. Above is a medieval warrior arrayed in chain mail.

29

him a hunchbacked son, whose deformity would prevent him from succeeding his father. Charles accepted his mother's plan, much to the alarm of the Pope, who feared an alliance between his supporters, the Franks, and his enemies, "the perfidious and stinking Lombards," as he called them in the forthright language of the age. "Saint Peter himself, prince of the apostles, guardian of the keys to the Kingdom of Heaven . . . ," the Pope wrote to Charles, "by all that is lawful, by the living and true God, by the ineffable divine omnipotence, by the tremendous day of judgment, by all the divine mysteries . . . adjures you not to wed the daughter of Desiderius. . . ." Should he ignore the Pontiff's solemn ban, Charles would be "doomed with the devil and his most wicked ministers and all impious men to the eternal flames."

As a faithful son of the Church, Charles was certainly distressed by the Pope's condemnation of the marriage. He also apparently did not like the nameless Lombard princess, for reasons that are veiled by the sources. Within a year Charles repudiated her. To the great indignation of the Lombards he sent her back to her father and married a Frankish girl of his own choice. Hildigard, the third of his five wives, was then little more than a child. She was to bear him five daughters and four sons and to form the center of the family life that Charles came to love more than war and conquest.

The divorce of the Lombard princess was a sign that Queen Bertrada's influence over her elder son was waning. And as Charles more and more asserted his independence of his mother, the tensions between the two brothers rose. Throughout the year 771 there were rumors of impending war between Charles and Carloman. Probably only Charles' good luck averted it. For luck can be as much a part of greatness as will and intelligence, and in Charles' case an untimely death proved to be a stroke of good fortune for him. At the end of 771 his brother died after a brief illness. In those days of primitive medicine there were few remedies for disease, and all the contemporary sources make it plain that Carloman died a natural death. Charles' reaction to it was natural too, though possibly not altogether legal. He took possession of his brother's kingdom

A page from the book in which the illustration opposite appears offers a fine example of Carolingian minuscule. Just then coming into vogue, the clear, cursive script served as a model for Renaissance lettering, the basis of modern type.

Exotic birds, and the stag often linked to baptism, flock to the Fountain of Life (left), a representation of the Church in a gospel book prepared at Mainz between 781 and 783 for Charlemagne and his wife, Hildigard.

LOMBARD TREASURES

In the year 568 the Lombards set fire to their old homes in what is now Yugoslavia and crossed the Alps into Italy; within a few years they were masters of half the peninsula. Only the weak power of the Pope at Rome and the Byzantine Emperor's Exarch at Ravenna separated their northern possessions —still called Lombardy—and their southern duchies of Spoleto and Benevento (see map, pages 72–73). But it was the land that came to shape the people. When conquered two centuries later by the Franks, these former wanderers were in the process of becoming Italians. Originally Arians, members of a heretical Christian sect, they were then subject to Rome, and Latin speech was replacing their Germanic tongue. The transformation of a barbaric society can be seen in these Lombard treasures.

On the crude gilded copper plate below, part of a helmet decoration, Lombard King Agilulf (590–615) appears as the conqueror receiving tribute. His wife, Theodelinda, had more refined tastes. An early Catholic, the Queen corresponded with Pope Gregory the Great and received from him such gifts as the elaborate book binding opposite. The ninth-century Iron Crown of Lombardy below it—so called for the strip of iron inside, said to be from a nail of the True Cross—was worn by Charlemagne's successors as a symbol of his 774 conquest of the once powerful Lombards.

CATHEDRAL TREASURY, MONZA

NATIONAL MUSEUM, FLORENCE: PHOTO SCALA

CATHEDRAL TREASURY, MONZA

33

even though Carloman had two infant sons who might have inherited his throne—and thus further splintered Pepin's heritage. Well aware of the perils of a regency, the nobles of Carloman's half of the kingdom ratified the usurpation in a formal assembly. Although Charles' old tutor, Abbot Fulrad of St. Denis, organized a smooth transfer of power, some nobles objected and fled to Lombardy. Along with them went Carloman's wife, Gerberga, and her two sons. Her flight was foolish, Charles commented, for he would not have harmed them. But he undoubtedly would have placed his brother's sons in a monastery for life.

With Carloman's realm added to his own, Charles now ruled virtually all of present-day France, Belgium, and the Netherlands; a part of western Germany; and some of Switzerland (see map, pages 72–73). He was also overlord of Bavaria. Duke Tassilo of Bavaria—Charles' cousin, a young man his own age—had once sworn homage to the "three kings of the Franks," namely to Pepin, Charles, and Carloman. In fact, however, Tassilo had always asserted his independence, and Bavaria could not really be counted as part of the Frankish realm. The status of Bavaria was one element in the unfinished business that King Pepin had left to his sons: the duties that now fell to Charles alone. He would have to deal with it some day, but at this early stage in his reign he preferred to let the matter rest. The question of Bavaria was complicated by marital alliances; for Duke

The gods of Charlemagne's pagan opponents often had surprisingly long histories. The Gundestrup Caldron, a first-century-B.C. silver vessel discovered in Denmark, featured the antlered figure of Cernunnos (left), holding a serpent. The same god reappears in a ninth-century Psalter (right), his headdress now of feathers but still carrying a snake. One soul escaping hell kisses the foot of his Saviour, Christ, who has just pulled another through the gate, guarded by a menacing Cernunnos.

Tassilo's wife was a daughter of King Desiderius of Lombardy and the sister of the Lombard princess whom Charles had just married and divorced.

Divided, Frankland had been weak, although Charles in conquering Aquitaine had behaved as if it were strong. But now, with the resources of the whole Frankish kingdom at his disposal, he felt that he could set about those tasks of conquest and civilizing that were to be the hallmark of his reign. He attended first to the area of greatest danger. That was the ill-defined Saxon border to the north of Austrasia, as the old heartland of the Frankish realm was called.

The Saxons, Continental relatives of those Saxons who had conquered Britain in the fifth and sixth centuries, were still pagans. This does not imply that they were savages. They had a complex mythology, a priesthood, regular rites, and they worshiped a pantheon of gods who resembled, although they were not identical with, the gods of the Greeks and the Romans. Like the Greeks, they had sacred groves where they celebrated many of their religious ceremonies; these groves were as sanctified to them as churches were to the Christians. But some of their practices were deeply shocking to Christians. Occasionally, as the early Greeks had done, they still performed human sacrifices, and it was alleged that they sometimes practiced ritual cannibalism.

Anglo-Saxon missionaries from England, who spoke their language, had gone among the Saxons trying to con-

35

vert them to Christianity. These missionaries had received financial support and sometimes military escorts from the Frankish kings, but they had had small success. The Saxons either martyred them or drove them away and continued to live by their old gods, Thunar, Woden, and Saxnot. Moreover, they regarded the settlements of their Christian, Frankish neighbors as fair game for pillage.

Much of the border between Saxony and Frankland lay in open plain and had fluctuated for many years according to the fortunes of war. The Saxons lived in a tribal society, uniting only briefly for the purpose of raiding their more settled neighbors. In the past they had seldom been a match for Frankish armies in the open field. But they were masters of ambush and guerrilla warfare; and during the

Like Boniface, Willibrord left his native England for missionary work on the Continent. The saint, depicted at left with two disciples, died in 738 and was buried in Luxembourg, where miracles worked in his name were already being reported in Charles' time. The Frisians, among whom Willibrord worked, two decades later gave Boniface a martyr's death.

36

three years the Frankish kingdom had been divided between Charles and Carloman, they had grown bolder and more predatory. Now that Frankland was reunited, Charles resolved to punish their insults to Christian missionaries and their burning of Christian churches. In the spring of 772 he called an assembly of the Franks at Worms, a city located on the Upper Rhine River, and persuaded his nobles to vote for war against the Saxons. The Frankish warriors did not need much persuasion, for they were eager to try their arms under their new leader, and as always, were lured by the prospect of booty. But it is worth noting that deliberation of the assembly of notables was essential. Charles was by no means an absolute ruler who could begin a war without the consent of his people.

The summer campaign against the Saxons was an unqualified success from start to finish. It opened with the capture of a Saxon fortress called the Eresburg, near what is now Paderborn. Charles then advanced to a Saxon sacred grove where Thunar, Woden, and Saxnot were worshiped at a great pillar (or perhaps an ancient tree trunk) called the Irminsul. As at a Christian sanctuary, there were houses for the priests and treasures of silver and gold around the fane. Charles and his army marched so swiftly that the Saxons had no time to remove their treasures to safety. To the considerable satisfaction of the fighting men, the Franks took large quantities of booty. They then proceeded to topple the Irminsul and destroy all the surrounding buildings.

After spending three days doing a thorough job of desecration, Charles and his men marched through Saxony to the Weser River, burning and pillaging as they went. Because the Saxons were not ready for pitched battle with the full force of the Franks, the invaders met no substantial resistance. At the Weser a parley was arranged; the Saxons gave twelve hostages for good behavior, and the Franks returned home. Charles chose to accept their promises and to grant easy terms, because he had other pressing problems—among them, probably, his desire to return to Hildigard before she gave birth to their first son.

With the prestige of his Saxon victories behind him, Charles had little difficulty in convincing his subjects that the Kingdom of the Franks must intervene in the affairs of Italy. Once more he was to take up his father's unfinished business. The Lombards had resumed their encroachments upon the lands of the Holy See, and the new Pope, Hadrian I, appealed to Charles for aid against the new Lombard

With fierce pagans at their country's borders, Frankish Christians must often have thought of martyrdom. A scribe working on a late-eighth-century manuscript decorated the margin with the portrait above of St. Agatha, a third-century Christian martyr in Sicily.

King, Desiderius, as a former pope had appealed to Charles' father for aid against a former Lombard king. After twenty years the positions of the papacy, the Lombards, and the Franks were once more much the same.

But Charles was not his father; and wherever he took up programs that his father had begun, he carried them to a successful conclusion and transformed triumphs on the battlefield into permanent acquisitions. So it was now with the invasion of Lombardy. The war appeared to be a repetition of King Pepin's campaigns of 754 and 756. Although few of them were mountain men, the Franks breached the terrifying barrier of the Alps and pursued the retreating Lombards to the walled city of Pavia. But at this point Charles departed from his father's precedent.

He had observed with keen interest that most of the Lombard towns he encountered on his march surrendered to him without resistance. Their loyalty to King Desiderius was certainly less than fanatical, and Charles quickly grasped the reason. The bulk of the population consisted of "Romans"—that is, native Italians with whom the Germanic Lombards had intermarried and partly merged in the course of two centuries. The local chieftains did not seem to care who ruled them, so long as they were permitted to govern their own towns. They would submit to Frankish overlordship, Charles concluded, perhaps more readily than they would to their own Lombard king. In these circumstances Charles had the vision to see himself as King of the Lombards, and he promptly set about converting vision into reality.

King Desiderius was safely surrounded in Pavia. The Frankish army settled down for a nine-month-long siege; Charles was not inclined to waste men's lives attempting to storm a fortified city. But he also did not like to sit idle. Leaving part of his army to maintain the siege, he continued to march down the Po River Valley. Charles received the surrender of one city after the other, until all of Lombardy, except for Pavia, was in his hands. Then he turned his face south, toward the heart of Christendom and the ancient capital of the world: Rome.

Rome in the third quarter of the eighth century was no longer the great metropolis of Augustus Caesar. Its population had shrunk; its mighty monuments were falling to decay. But the ancient buildings had not yet been quarried for stone as they would be by the builders of a later age, and many of them still stood in nearly their original glory. For a king, Rome still held imperial memories; for a

Christian, it was above all a holy city, the residence of the pope, and the site of St. Peter's martyrdom and tomb, to which every Christian hoped to make a pilgrimage some day. For Charles, to be in Rome at Easter was an act of religious dedication and political wisdom. At the end of March, 774, accompanied by a brilliant retinue of his nobles and clerics, Charles approached the Eternal City.

He had not announced his coming to Pope Hadrian, who learned of it almost at the last minute. But the Pope hastily prepared a magnificent welcome for the conqueror of Lombardy and savior of the papacy. All of official Rome journeyed to a point thirty miles outside the city to hail Charles. Along the final mile leading to Rome, children, waving branches of palm and olive and singing hymns,

A mounted host storms a walled city in this scene from the Utrecht Psalter, a psalmbook made about 832 near the French city of Reims. Although they illustrate Biblical events, the volume's animated pen drawings—the most brilliant of this early period—vividly reflect the spirit of medieval life.

39

Charles (third from left) and his attendants meet the Pope in this Belgian manuscript illustration. The historic meeting takes place in the somewhat cramped quarters of a church perhaps meant to be Rome's vast St. Peter's Basilica.

lined the road. At St. Peter's Basilica the Pope awaited Charles at the top of the steps; and Charles, like any pilgrim, fell to his knees and kissed each step as he ascended.

During his first few days in Rome the King of the Franks continued to behave like a pilgrim. On Easter Sunday, the day after his arrival, he saw the Holy Crib at Santa Maria Maggiore, attended the papal Mass, and went sight-seeing elsewhere in Rome. He saw the Colosseum, still in use for bullfights; visited the spot where St. Peter was crucified; and paid his respects to St. Peter at the very tomb of the Apostle. But in the midst of the religious ceremonies, the feasting, and the entertainment, Charles also had time for talks with Pope Hadrian about more mundane matters. He took the measure of the handsome Pope, who was a true Roman aristocrat of ancient family, and found that he liked him. A genuine friendship, which was to endure for twenty years, sprang up between the young King and the middle-aged Pontiff.

Charles, however, never permitted friendship to dictate policy. Pope Hadrian wanted to increase the "patrimony of St. Peter," the territory under the aegis of the Holy See. Since the Lombard power had now been crushed, he asked for the entire Exarchate of Ravenna, the provinces of Venetia and Istria, the duchies of Spoleto and Benevento, and the island of Corsica—that is, for most of Italy except Lombardy. Charles was willing to be generous, but as conqueror of Lombardy, he was unwilling to give away lands he now regarded as his own. Far from granting the Pope's demands, he merely confirmed the Donation of Pepin and perhaps (the exact terms of the agreement have been lost) added some territory to it.

With a feeling on both sides that a new era of collaboration between the Roman Church and the Frankish kingdom had begun, but also with some dissatisfaction on the Pope's part, Charles took his leave of Hadrian. He returned to the siege of Pavia, and within a month—by June, 774—the city surrendered. King Desiderius was consigned to a Frankish monastery for life, and Charles took possession of his treasure and his crown. At the age of thirty-two Charles was King of the Franks and the Lombards—*Rex Francorum et Langobardorum*. The wealth of the rich cities of the Po plain was at his disposal. Already he held more power than any other ruler in Europe except the Eastern Roman emperor at Constantinople. And he was only at the beginning of his astonishing career.

For a few months Charles lingered in Italy, consolidating the conquest. He received the submissions of local Lombard lords and left them undisturbed in possession of their towns and lands. Later he would place among them a sprinkling of Frankish nobles to insure their loyalty. But for the present he was feeling his way in a strange land; he took care not to arouse hostility by hasty interference with local government and customs.

When the summer heat descended upon Italy, he set out for the north. The Saxons had profited by his absence, raiding deep into Frankish territory, and Charles had to launch a punitive expedition once again. While he crossed the Alps with the main body of the army, he sent a small contingent on a forced march ahead. These troops caught the Saxon raiders by surprise and drove them in disorder out of Frankish territory. Then the Franks in turn invaded Saxony, burning and plundering for a while before they withdrew.

Such operations could be repeated indefinitely, but Charles was not content—as the Frankish rulers before his time had been—to engage in interminable warfare on his borders. Warrior though he was, his real interest lay in peaceful construction, in prosperous farms, good roads, thriving towns, fine churches, and a secure, stable life for his people. Such conditions seemed impossible as long as

BRITISH MUSEUM: HARLEY ROLL Y 6

Men entering monasteries had the tops of their heads tonsured, or shaved, as a symbol of their withdrawal from worldly life. Above, a bishop with a pair of scissors clips the hair of a kneeling man.

This twelfth-century tombstone sculpture shows Widukind as the pacified Christian he was to become rather than as the intrepid leader of the pagan Saxons who gave Charlemagne such trouble.

the border was harried by predatory pagans. If he could Christianize the Saxons, he decided, they would be more likely to live in peace with their Frankish neighbors. That fall and winter of 775 he decided that the Saxons must be converted to Christianity. As the Frankish annals put it, he resolved "to wage war upon the perfidious and oath-breaking Saxon people until they were conquered and converted to the Christian religion, or totally annihilated."

In the course of the next thirty years that fearful vow very nearly did lead to the annihilation of the Saxon people. Saxony was repeatedly subdued by the overwhelming might of Frankish arms. But Charles found it impossible to win over the Saxon people. Time and again he cowed them into temporary submission, only to find guerrilla bands springing up everywhere as soon as the Frankish troops left the country. As fighters the Saxons were the equals of the Franks, and they had the natural advantage that "barbarians" always have over advanced nations: they had much less to lose. They had no cities to be destroyed; their wattle huts could easily be rebuilt if burned; and they could safely hide their cattle and horses, which constituted most of their property, in the dense forests and trackless marshes of their homeland. They knew the country, knew the few safe paths through the swamps; and they fought and traveled with few of the impediments of an organized army.

The very threat of Frankish conquest, moreover, helped the Saxons to overcome their greatest weakness: disunity. At the time the Frankish assault began, Saxony was divided into hundreds of districts, with many local chiefs but no king or other leader. Under Frankish pressure, however, a nobleman named Widukind began rallying his fellow Saxons for a sustained effort against the Franks. Brave and intelligent, related by marriage to the King of the Danes, Widukind seemed to Charles to have the dangerous potential for founding a kingdom of Saxony.

It was not natural to Charles' generally kindly temperament to decide upon what today would be called genocide. Nor was it a wise decision, as the event proved. In his later dealings with the Saxons he learned that a lenient and conciliatory policy yielded results and that blood and iron only stiffened the Saxon resistance. But in 775 he was still young, impatient, somewhat unsure of himself, and alarmed at the possibility of an alliance between the Saxons and his cousin Tassilo's Bavarians. As ruler of Gaul and Italy, his position toward the Germans on his borders resembled that of the Roman emperors; he had to be per-petually on guard against a "barbarian" influx. But he was also a devout Christian who believed that in convert-ing the Saxons he was engaged in God's work. The fact that converted Saxons were alienated from their own people, and indeed regarded as traitors by other Saxons, also aided the conquest by furthur dividing the enemy. Priests and missionaries, therefore, followed close behind the Frankish armies whenever they advanced into Saxony.

The army penetrated deeply in the course of the next two years, and large numbers of Saxons submitted to bap-tism under the menace of the sword. By the late spring of 777 Charles thought that Saxony had been sufficiently sub-dued for him to hold the annual assembly of the Franks at Paderborn, in southern Saxony. The Saxons of the sub-jugated territories were ordered to attend, and many of them came to take loyalty oaths and to be baptized. Con-vinced that Saxony was firmly in hand, Charles decided that he could turn his attention to other matters. He listened with interest to a group of ambassadors from across the Pyrenees—and allowed himself to be lured into one of the few great fiascoes of his reign.

Another version of the siege war-fare Charlemagne used against his enemies appears in this eleventh-century drawing. The commander has divided his forces into infantry archers (top) and cavalry for a two-pronged attack on the city.

43

In another scene from the late-fourteenth-century manuscript Grandes Chroniques de France, *a solemn, white-bearded Charles receives a Moslem embassy seeking his intervention in Spain. Behind the kneeling Moor at center stand three stylized camels, one apparently carrying a water tank.*

III

DEFEAT AND RECOVERY

The embassy that waited on Charles at Paderborn in 777 was headed by ibn-al-Arabi, the Saracen, or Moslem, governor of Barcelona. In the middle of the eighth century the Umayyad dynasty, which had ruled Islam from the Syrian city of Damascus for nearly a hundred years, had been overthrown by the descendants of Abbas, Mohammed's uncle. The Abbassides, as the new dynasty was called, hunted down every Umayyad with savage determination, slaughtering the members of the old dynasty wherever they were found. A single Umayyad named Abd-er-Rahman survived the massacre. Escaping to Spain, the far western outpost of the Arab world, Abd-er-Rahman established himself as emir of Córdoba, ruler of those Moslems still loyal to the old dynasty. Feeling between the two factions ran so high that the Abbasside Saracens in Spain preferred an alliance with Christians to submission to other Moslems. Ibn-al-Arabi therefore came to ask Charles' help in overthrowing the last of the hated Umayyads.

Charles was attracted by the prospect of freeing the Christians of Spain from the Moslem yoke, for the tradition of combating the Saracens was strong in his family. His grandfather Charles Martel (The Hammer) had checked the fearful Moslem thrust into France at the Battle of Tours in 732. His father, Pepin, had completed the work by driving the Saracens back across the Pyrenees Mountains. Perhaps Charles himself, now that the infidels were quarreling among themselves, could reconquer all of Spain for Christianity. Undoubtedly, he thought, the entire Christian population of Spain, subjugated by the Moslems little more than sixty years earlier, would rise up in arms and join forces with an invading Christian army.

Acting on these assumptions, Charles assembled, by late spring of 778, one of the largest military forces that had ever been seen in Frankland. In addition to his own Franks, he levied, or won by promise of booty, large contingents of

In a detail from Chartres Cathedral's famous windows, Charles sets off on horseback for Spain.

The Frankish hero Roland, at left in this depiction of the Battle of Roncesvalles, smites a mounted opponent with his ponderous sword. The twelfth-century stone relief adorns the Cathedral of St. Pierre at Angoulême in western France.

Lombards, Burgundians, Romans, Bavarians, and Goths. Two army corps, under the command of his chief nobles, marched through the passes of the Pyrenees—one corps at the Mediterranean end and the other, led by Charles himself, at the western, or Atlantic, end of the range.

But the grand project encountered unexpected difficulties from the start. The Christian Basques of Navarre, far from welcoming Charles, fought to defend their independence. In fact, the Christian subjects of the Moslem emirate appeared to be quite content with their tolerant Saracen overlords. The Abbasside faction had overestimated its own strength; and ibn-al-Arabi proved unable to deliver the fortress-city of Saragossa to the Franks, as he had promised. Charles could advance no farther than the Ebro River; then he was forced to retreat, for reasons that the annals obscure. Possibly word reached him while he was still in Spain that the Saxons were gathering a large army on his northern border and were once again preparing to take advantage of his absence. At any rate, he withdrew with his dream of reconquering Spain for Christianity unfulfilled.

On the return march to Frankland there took place a small skirmish that was destined to become one of the most famous battles in the history of the world. The Frankish forces paused at the Navarrese city of Pampeluna, where Charles punished the Christian inhabitants for their resistance to him by razing the walls of the city. In early August he continued on through the pass in the Pyrenees at Roncesvalles. The Basques stationed at Roncesvalles waited until the bulk of the army had passed through the narrow defile between high mountains, then fell upon Charles' rear guard and baggage train. They fired arrows from ambush and rolled huge stones down upon the Franks, whose mobility was hampered by their heavy armor. As Einhard, the biographer of Charlemagne, tells the story:

In the battle that followed the Gascons [Basques] killed their opponents to the last man. Then they seized the baggage and under cover of night scattered with the greatest speed in different directions. . . . In this battle Eggihard, the royal seneschal; Anselm, count of the palace; and Hruodland, warden of the Breton frontier, were killed along with very many others.

It was a Frankish defeat, and Charlemagne's biographer did not elaborate. However, the imagination of the

An unintentionally humorous manuscript illumination records the knighting of Roland. Two attendants attaching spurs to the diminutive warrior's ankles appear to be lifting Roland so that tall, stately King Charles can present him with a sword. The bishop at right blesses Roland as a servant (left) wrestles with an armful of swords, perhaps to be given to other knights in the same ceremony.

In this fourteenth-century Italian manuscript illumination, Frankish warriors scramble

into their armor as Roland (right) sounds a horn announcing the approach of the enemy.

common people was kindled by the dramatic circumstances of the battle: the frowning mountain peaks, the victory of craft over power, the heroism of a struggle to the last man, the fame of some of the men who were killed. Sixty years later an early-ninth-century writer declared that he need not list again the names of those who fell in the pass at Roncesvalles, because everybody already knew who they were. Songs and legendary embroiderings of the episode appeared almost immediately. In time the name of Count Roland (Hruodland)—who in fact was a sufficiently important official to strike his own coins—became familiar to every man and woman in Western Europe. In the course of the next three centuries the story was pieced together by one or several great minstrels into *The Song of Roland* (*Chanson de Roland*), one of the glories of medieval literature. The real and comparatively trivial incident at Roncesvalles remains important only for the work of art it produced.

How much historical truth *The Song of Roland* relates we shall never know. Charlemagne himself is pictured as he was known to the later Middle Ages, white-haired and already Emperor, uncle of Roland (which he was not), and deceived by the traitor Ganelon, who successfully plots the

Incidents from The Song of Roland *are depicted in three scenes from the* Grandes Chroniques de France. *At left, St. James appears to a sleeping Charlemagne, asking the Frankish ruler to liberate his Spanish tomb from the Moslems. Opposite, top, Roland charges full tilt at the dusky-skinned Moors. Opposite, below, the slain hero lies on the battlefield, as two angels bear his sainted soul toward the light of heaven.*

BIBLIOTHÈQUE NATIONALE, SERVICE PHOTOGRAPHIQUE: MS. FR. 2813 FOL. 118 v

BIBLIOTHÈQUE NATIONALE, SERVICE PHOTOGRAPHIQUE: MS. FR. 2813 FOL. 122 v

destruction of his rival Roland. The Basques are transformed by the *Song* into Saracens. But there is very likely historical fact behind the depiction of Roland's pride: not until all his men lie dead upon the field does he sound his horn to signal the rest of the army that he needs help. And there is surely a memory of the true history in the wonderful description of Charlemagne's grief when he returns to the pass to find that he can do nothing but bury his dead, for the enemy has completely vanished:

In Roncesvalles Charles now has set his feet,
And for the dead he finds begins to weep. . . .
He sees his nephew lying on green grass.
No wonder, then, that Charles is full of wrath.
Dismounts and goes to him; his heart is sad.
He holds the count between his own two hands
And on the body faints, so sharp's the pang. . . .

"My friend Roland, God lay your soul on flowers,
In Paradise with all the glorious host.
You came to Spain with a cruel overlord.
No day shall pass henceforth that I'll not mourn."

The Song of Roland depicts Charlemagne as returning to Spain for revenge and slaughtering the pagans by the thousands. But in fact Charles never went near Spain in person again. In later years he sent his generals across the Pyrenees, and over many years of fighting in Spain they carved out a strip of territory that ran across the peninsula just north and west of Barcelona. This was called the Spanish March (from the old Germanic word *Mark*, meaning "border"); it remained a kind of buffer territory between Moslem Spain and Christian Frankland. But Charles had nothing like the revenge pictured in song and legend; he returned home saddened and embittered. For the first time in the ten years of his rule he had met with reverses.

The reverses did not come singly. At Auxerre, in central France, Charles heard the news that the Saxons had broken their oaths and had risen again. During his absence they had made a savage hit-and-run raid across the border, burning and plundering as far as the Rhine. It was too late in the year for a campaign in Saxony proper; Charles could do no more than send a few detachments of his disbanding army to drive them back across the border. Then he tried to take stock of his own situation and that of his kingdom and to forge plans for the coming decade.

By this time Hildigard, the girl-bride whom Charles had married after divorcing the Lombard princess, had

Frankish knights killed at Roncesvalles topple to the ground like a row of falling dominoes in this detail from Charlemagne's shrine at Aachen. At far right, the King in his palace weeps at the news of his army's severe losses.

ISLAMIC SPAIN

The Moslems Charles encountered in Spain had achieved their astonishing conquest of the Iberian Peninsula in just eight years early in the eighth century. After the failure of the Frankish King's efforts to drive them back to North Africa, the Saracens continued to dominate Spanish life for another four centuries; indeed, the last Moors were not driven from Spanish soil until 1492. However, the long occupation left Spain a rich artistic legacy. The Great Mosque at Córdoba (left), begun in 785 by Abd-er-Rahman, rises in colorful horseshoe arches from 850 Roman columns. Made two centuries later for another Córdoban prince, the intricately carved ivory box at right features a musician playing a lute, an Arab import from Persia. A fine record of Moslem life is preserved in thirteenth-century manuscripts made at the court of Castile and León. The detail below, in which two Moorish chieftains in a tent ponder chess moves, is from the first European description of the Oriental game.

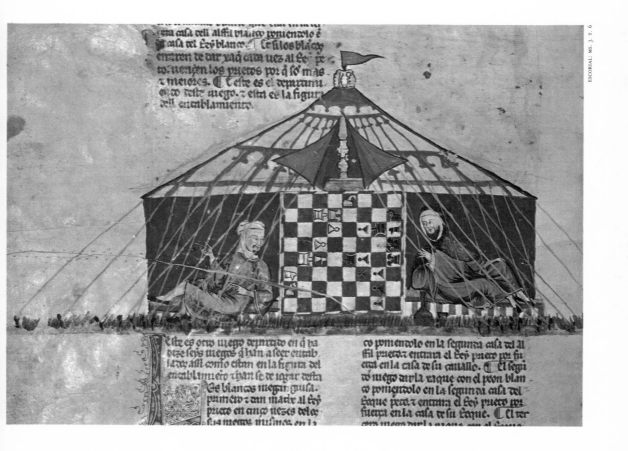

Pen and inkpot in hand, a medieval scribe copies a manuscript —slow, painstaking work, as can be seen by his intent posture. His tonsure, or shaved head, denotes membership in a monastic order.

given Charles four sons: Charles, Carloman, and during the summer of 778 a pair of twins, Louis and Lothar, of whom only Louis survived. There was also, at the court but not really a member of it, Charles' son by his first wife: Pepin the Hunchback, who was cut off from the succession. There were, in addition, several daughters. Charles was thus surrounded by the bustle of a growing family, and by all accounts he delighted in it. During this period in his life he began to devote much more of his attention than ever before to the domestic conditions of his country and to creating around himself the atmosphere proper to a great king's court. He became a patron of the arts. Painters, silversmiths, goldsmiths, ivory carvers, manuscript illuminators, sculptors, and men of letters began swarming to his court like bees to honey, drawn by the lavishness with which Charles treated artists and men of learning and by the opportunity to exchange ideas with other scholars and craftsmen.

Cultivated kings had once been no novelty among the Franks. In Merovingian times King Chilperic had written poems, and other Merovingian monarchs had encouraged building and the arts of embellishment. The traditions of Roman secular society had persisted into the fifth and sixth centuries. In spite of the "barbarian" invasions, there remained schools for laymen, and at least the upper and middle classes were largely literate. But during the upheavals of the first half of the eighth century, that tradition of secular learning had been ruptured. Society in Frankland approached the state that old-fashioned writers regarded as characteristic of the medieval period—a state in which all learning and literacy were concentrated among the clergy. In actuality some tradition of secular culture continued all through the period between the fall of Rome and the Renaissance; for whenever learning threatened to become entirely extinguished, enlightened rulers, such as Charlemagne, would revive it.

Charles began with himself. Political setbacks had turned his thoughts toward philosophy and religion. Seized by a passion for learning, the king began studying grammar like a schoolboy and even took lessons in astronomy and music. Some of the time that he had formerly given to hunting and hawking (although he continued these favorite pastimes also) Charles now spent on studying the Bible and the writings of the Church Fathers. He began gathering around himself a company of established scholars and bright young men, among whom he sought the equality of intellectual exchange. This group of poets, grammarians, astronomers, mathematicians, musicians, architects, theologians, and philosophers adopted the rather quaint habit of addressing one another by pseudonyms taken from the classical or scriptural traditions. Even women participated; Charles' sister, Gisla, bore the nickname of Lucia; his daughter Rotrud was known as Columba. Bishop Theodulf of Orleans, a fine poet, was called Pindar, and another good poet, Charles' chaplain Angilbert, bore the name of Homer. King Charles himself was known as David, and illustrations of King David in early Carolingian art have been taken as portraits of Charlemagne.

Scholars flocked to the court of the Frankish King from all over Europe. Such men as Peter of Pisa, who gave Charles lessons in grammar, and Paulinus (whom Charles later appointed Patriarch of Aquileia) had been noted for their scholarship before they became courtiers in Frankland. Paul the Deacon was to write his chief work, the *History of the Lombards*, after he left the court of Charles and retired to the quiet monastic life of Monte Cassino. Irish scholars, such as Dungal and Clement, began a program of systematic astronomical observation for the King, who took an enthusiastic interest in the engrossing science of the heavens.

The great luminary among the learned men of Charlemagne's court was an Englishman by birth, Alcuin. Schooled in the classics at the famous cathedral school at York, Alcuin had become its director and won for himself the reputation of being one of the finest scholars of his age. He commanded an elegant, if imitative, Latin style, held strictly orthodox views in theology, excelled in rhetoric, and wrote a pleasant if undistinguished sort of poetry. But it was as a teacher that Alcuin achieved greatness. He had the rare quality of being able to inspire a passion for knowledge. His pupils were scattered all over England and the Continent, and they clung to him with lifelong loyalty. He was not creative, in the modern sense of the term; for he thought it enough to pass on the doctrines of the Fathers of the Church and the wisdom of the great Roman writers to the next generation. But that was a vital task for Frankland, where even in the monasteries mere literacy was not always securely established. Alcuin was also a careful textual critic, and that, too, was crucial in a land where the textbooks had been corrupted because the copying of them had been left to the ignorant, semiliterate monks and boys who inhabited the monasteries.

Charlemagne (left) hails Alcuin's wisdom as a gift of God in this late-twelfth-century manuscript detail, the only known medieval representation of the noted scholar. The long scrolls they hold record their conversation, much as do balloons in modern comic strips.

Alcuin became a close friend of Charles, combining the roles of teacher, theological expert, and general repository of knowledge. But he was more than that, for he also served Charles as a sort of minister of education. There was no regularly organized cabinet in Charles' government; but in an informal way the men who were constant members of his court assumed different functions according to their talents and the need. As schoolmaster of the country, so to speak, Alcuin conducted the palace school for the children of the sovereign and the courtiers. He encouraged the expansion of existing schools in monasteries and cathedrals throughout the country. Ultimately he probably envisioned —although he was never able to carry this policy to fruition —a kind of universal free education for all boys. (The education of women was never formally provided for in Frank-

CONVENT OF SAN PAOLO FUORI LE MURA, ROME

land, although there were a number of very well-educated women in the country.) Alcuin also began accumulating a library for Charles. He edited existing textbooks and wrote a number of his own. In addition, he advised Charles on political matters—most notably when he recommended a far more lenient treatment of the Saxons than Charles had hitherto practiced. The learned churchman finally spent much time combating the religious heresies that sprang up in parts of the Frankish Empire toward the end of the century.

In his later years Alcuin longed for retirement from the hurly-burly of court life, and at last Charles granted his wish by making him Abbot of Tours, one of the richest monasteries in Frankland. There Alcuin devoted himself to enlarging the *scriptoria*, as the writing rooms of monasteries

The method of copying manuscripts to preserve ancient learning for later generations is revealed in the illustration below, from a late-ninth-century Bible made for one of Charlemagne's successors. St. Jerome, author of the Latin version of the Bible, is shown at left, dictating to four scribes. At right, the monks store their completed volumes in the monastery library, which strangely looks like nothing more than a farm silo.

were called. He employed large numbers of monks in the patient labor of copying manuscripts. He also fostered the development of the Carolingian minuscule, the handwriting that King Charles himself tried so hard to learn. So successful was Alcuin in furthering the work of copyists, by urging and example, that we owe to him and his immediate successors much of what we know of the ancient world. Ninety per cent of Latin writings have come down to us in Carolingian copies or copies of such copies.

In addition to concerning himself with education, Charles sought to improve the small matters of daily life throughout his kingdoms. As he traveled about his realm or set out on military campaigns, he found the condition of the roads deplorable and began to devote part of his growing resources to road building. By tradition the people whose lands bordered a road were responsible for its upkeep. Charles now issued decrees declaring the tradition a law; and he made a point of enforcing it. He likewise encouraged the construction of new bridges; the builders were allowed to charge tolls.

There was no regular system of finance in the Frankish kingdom. The revenues of the king came from the royal estates called "vills," which comprised a manor house or palace and the surrounding lands. These vills had at times been administered in a highly haphazard manner, with most of the profits going to the stewards or being diverted from the royal treasury in other ways. Sometimes stewards had mercilessly squeezed the peasants who toiled on the estates, or else they had allowed buildings to fall into disrepair. Charles, a good husbandman in small matters as well as large, put an end to negligence and cheating. His decree concerning the management of the royal vills has been preserved, and it presents an altogether remarkable picture of the conditions and needs of the times, the agricultural practices, and the close, almost pedantic sense of detail possessed by Charles the Great.

As we read the decree, we can almost see Charles going about his vills with the stewards, paying attention to the way lard is extracted; meat smoked and salted; wine, cheese, and butter made. Everywhere, Charles insisted that food be prepared "with the greatest cleanliness"—even

The cutaway picture of a monastery at right shows three monks at work in a second-story scriptorium next to a bell tower. The instruments they hold were for trimming and measuring pages and steadying vellum while copying.

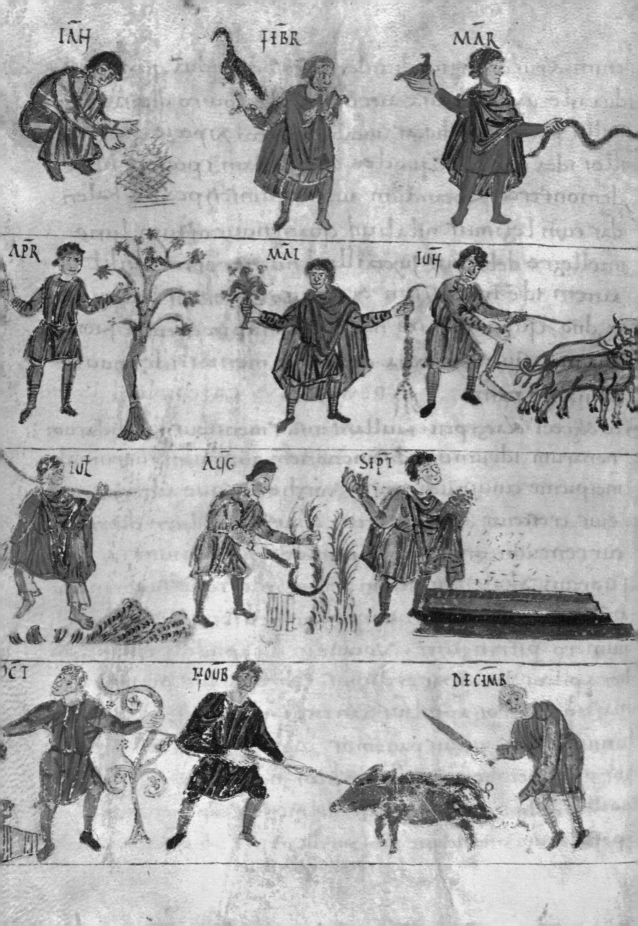

The annual round of activities in Carolingian times is recorded in the early-ninth-century illustration at left. The labors of the months start with January's hovering over a fire and February's sport of hawking, through springtime's planting, July and August's reaping, to an autumn boar hunt. At right, another seasonal chore: cleaning out a giant wine barrel.

forbidding the picturesque if unhygienic custom of treading grapes into wine with bare feet. He reproved his stewards for postponing necessary repairs until buildings had to be replaced. He regulated beekeeping, fruit raising, and seed selection, saw to the stocking of his fish ponds, and even went so far as to mention the seventy-four types of vegetables and herbs he wanted cultivated in his gardens. But he concerned himself with beauty as well as utility. He decreed that flowers must be grown on the estates to give pleasure to the eye and to provide for decorating the altars of the churches; swans, pheasants, peacocks, and other birds must be kept "for the sake of ornament."

There were royal estates throughout Frankland, and Charles obviously could not visit all of them in the course of one, two, or even five years. Neither could he travel through all the provinces, let alone all the countries of his realm, at frequent intervals. Yet his was an age of slow communications and personal government; where the hand of the master could not be felt, affairs did not go well. Charles could easily see this in the case of his estates, where year after year he tried to pound the elements of bookkeeping into the heads of stupid, stubborn, or sly stewards. He could see it also at the Franks' great annual spring assemblies, which all the nobles and higher clergy were required to attend. At these Marchfields—or as they tended

COLLECTION OF DR. PETER AND IRENE LUDWIG: PHOTO, KRAUS RARE BOOKS

Charlemagne perfected the system of royal supervision over subordinate officials. In the scene at left, from a thirteenth-century Spanish law book, a medieval king warns the judge (right) not to accept bribes. The artist, perhaps bored with legal matters, added to the margin such playful details as a centaur shooting at a bird and a lean hound pursuing a hare.

to become under Charles' rule, Mayfields—many complaints against local officials were brought to Charles' notice. He would issue reprimands and order the offenders to mend their ways—only to learn at the next spring assembly that nothing had been done: such and such a bailiff was continuing to collect the Church tithe for his own benefit, or was demanding that his tenants pay more than their traditional share of the cost of his horse and armor, or had seized a widow's land, and so on.

To check these abuses and to extend the "sovereign's presence" to the remotest parts of his kingdoms, Charles began to employ his famous *missi dominici*, which means literally "the lord's emissaries." These royal commissioners, as they might be called, ultimately became one of the distinctive features of Carolingian government. The commissioners were given virtually royal powers—they appeared and spoke for the King. Each went about an assigned portion of the kingdom looking into the condition of his *missaticum*, as his territory was called. Very soon Charles made it a practice to send his *missi* out in pairs, one lay official and one member of the Church, so that together they could examine all aspects of society as well as keep an eye on one another. They held court, heard appeals, checked financial records, and in all ways acted as the King's eyes and ears, reporting directing to the King and seeing that his justice was done.

We do not know precisely when Charles first utilized the system of royal commissioners; but by the late 780's, the second decade of his reign, the *missi* were already going on regular rounds. The idea was borrowed from the Church's practice of having a bishop tour his see annually, inspecting the condition of its parishes. But the application of this idea to secular government seems to have been Charles' own inspiration, and it proved to be a great administrative innovation. Without the *missi*, Charles could scarcely have governed his far-flung realm with such success. Sometimes, of course, the *missi* could be bribed by the local lords and underlings they were supposed to judge. Charles soon learned that it was best to change the territory of commissioners frequently, to prevent them from forming close friendships in a region or profiting by the opportunity to cover up their own corruption. But no government system is ever safe from corruption. On the whole, the system worked well in Lombardy and Frankland, and it became an absolute necessity as soon as Charles began to enlarge his dominions. He was soon to do so by leaps and bounds. For after that brief setback on the Spanish frontier, the centralized power of the Franks expanded rapidly in all directions.

The vast differences between various levels of society in medieval times are shown in a fourteenth-century French manuscript. At top are the privileged churchmen and royalty—and the translator-scribe (center) who has slyly elevated himself to their status. Below, in descending order from left to right, are a falconer, a gentleman cavalier, a craftsman at his workbench, a farmer, and two serfs gnawing their humble fare.

65

cerui ce fluens tenui uelamine limbus

oncipit ingestas testis   tur gentibus auras

offer qc pedib, fonun

emin i[n]stabili sonipes feritate superbit

npatiens madidis frenarier ora lupatis

ic illuc frendens obuertit terga negata

bertate fuge · pressisq; timescit habenis

t hoc sese ostentans habitu uentosa uirago

Int utraq; acie supeminet · & falerium

Circuflectit equu uultu[q]; & uoce minat

IV

NEW CONQUESTS

Year after year Charles had been returning to Saxony, advancing farther to the north and east in each campaign and after each summer subjecting the conquered Saxons to forcible baptism. The Saxon upper classes, who owned land, cattle, and manor houses, soon realized that they had more to lose by opposing the Franks than by collaborating with them. Except for Widukind, paradoxically one of the wealthiest of them all, most nobles preferred to surrender and acknowledge Charles as their overlord. But Widukind, the Danish king's brother-in-law, continued to call for resistance. Returning to Saxony from his refuge in Denmark, he summoned the common people to a class war against their own nobles. Under his inspired leadership, all Saxony sprang to arms in a national uprising in 782. Saxon troops that Charles had drafted into the Frankish army deserted to their fellow countrymen. Before Charles could intervene personally, half of a sizable Frankish army was wiped out almost to the last man, and two of the foremost Frankish generals were killed.

Charles rushed to Süntel Mountain, the scene of the debacle, with fresh troops. But as at Roncesvalles, he found no enemy to punish. The Saxon army had disbanded; the guerrillas could no longer be distinguished from the local population. Furious with frustration, no longer able to think clearly, Charles committed the most frightful and dishonorable act of his life. He summoned all the chief men of Saxony to meet him at Verden on the Aller River, a short distance from the new city of Bremen, where Charles would soon establish an episcopal see. The Saxons came to Verden with their attendants, and Charles demanded the

Wielding battle axes, mounted warriors—the one at top using a lion skin as a saddle—charge foot soldiers in a spirited detail from a Carolingian manuscript. The exotic bird above forms the initial letter ''C'' in an early work.

Seventh-century bronze plaques found in Sweden show the hero of a Nordic saga pitted against wild beasts. Charlemagne's campaigns against the Saxons brought him into conflict with the non-Christian Danes, while his successors would be fighting other fierce Northmen.

names of the leaders of the rebellion. Widukind, whom all named, had again escaped to safety; but Charles forced the Saxons to denounce each other. Forty-five hundred nobles and commoners were condemned to death, and all were beheaded in a single day.

Charles showed no outward signs of remorse for this terrible crime; but there is evidence that he deeply repented it. To his shocked contemporaries the "slaughter of the Saxons," as it was called, meant that Charles had succumbed to the disease of kings, tyranny. Many of his own people who had cheerfully followed his lead in earlier years began to fear and resent his rule and even to plot against it. The act of intemperate violence, moreover, did not accomplish the purpose of frightening the Saxons into submission. On the contrary, it left among the Saxons so burning a hatred for the Franks that their resistance was to continue for another twenty years.

Charles and his contemporaries must have felt that Heaven itself was punishing him for the massacre at Verden. The following spring Charles' wife, Hildigard, died in childbirth, and her infant daughter, the last of her nine children, did not long survive her. Ten weeks later Charles lost his mother, Queen Bertrada. Although Charles married again after Hildigard's death, his new queen, Fastrada, was never liked. Somewhat unjustly, she was blamed for the harsh and cruel disposition that Charles displayed during those years of grim warfare against the Saxons.

Warfare it was. Previously, Charles had fought only campaigns in Saxony. But violence bred violence, as it always does, and the terrible slaughter at Verden stunned the Saxons for only a short while. Then, for the first time, all divisions among the Saxons ceased. Widukind was able to unite the entire country against the Franks. He even persuaded the seemingly long-Christianized Frisians to drive away their priests, resume worship of the old gods, and join him. The Saxons drove the Franks out of the strong points they had occupied, forcing them back upon the Frankish frontiers. Fighting raged back and forth in Westphalia and Eastphalia; the countryside between the Weser and the Rhine was devastated. Charles was compelled to keep his armies in the field in winter as well as summer; yet the resistance continued.

Charles had the advantage of numbers, superior arms, and vast resources. To provide the manpower for his far-ranging campaigns, he could call up men from the plains of Lombardy and the cities of Aquitaine and from the valleys of the Rhone, the Loire, the Seine, and the Meuse. But the embattled peasants of Saxony stood firm, although their crops went unharvested, their homes were burned, and their women and children were led away into captivity. Deserted by their own nobles, who submitted to the Franks, they fought on under the leadership of Widukind for three years.

In the end, the Saxon leader could no longer bear to witness the sufferings of his own people. After three years of bitter warfare, he consented to negotiate an end to the struggle. Yet even then it was Charles rather than Widukind who had to offer terms, for the endless war had strained the great resources of his kingdom. It had been exceedingly costly in men, in supplies, in needed work that was not done. If it continued much longer, Charles realized, it would totally ruin the class of freemen who were the backbone of the Frankish nation. His nobles were murmuring against the expense of fighting so far from their homes and against the pointlessness of a protracted war in which all booty had long since been consigned to the

The ferocity of hand-to-hand combat, such as that encountered by Charles in his repeated incursions into Saxony, was vividly depicted by an early-ninth-century artist. Spears, swords, and bows and arrows are used in the bitter clash.

flames. There was nothing left to be had in Saxony, nothing but death or mutilation in an ambush by an enemy who struck suddenly, then fled and vanished.

At the same time, the Frankish nobles could not refrain from admiring Widukind, who had fought so long against overwhelming odds. Many tales were told of his amazing escapes in hopeless situations. In one story he reversed the shoes on his horse and thus sent his pursuers dashing after him in the wrong direction. Especially among the Thuringians, who were near neighbors of the Saxons, Widukind had become something of a folk hero.

Charles desperately needed a negotiated peace. When he promised to withdraw his army completely from Saxony if Widukind would submit to him, the Saxon chief accepted the offer. After demanding hostages to ensure his safety,

The oath renouncing paganism, required of the Saxons at their conversion to Christianity, appears in an early-ninth-century manuscript (right, above). An illustration from the same period (right, below) reveals that baptism was often by total immersion—with one churchman anointing the convert and a second standing by with a handy towel. To remind him of the faith he was embracing, Charles' noted convert Widukind was given the portable reliquary at left, a valise-shaped container studded with precious jewels.

Widukind laid down his arms and was baptized into the Christian faith, with Charles himself standing sponsor at the baptism. Widukind repeated the formula of baptism that had been specially drawn up for Saxons: "I renounce the devil and all the devil's ilk and all the devil's works and words. And I renounce . . . Thunar and Woden and Saxnot and all the demons who are their companions. I believe in God, the Almighty Father. I believe in Christ, the Son of God. I believe in the Holy Spirit." Then Charles loaded his former enemy with gifts and requested Pope Hadrian to order three days of feasting and thanksgiving throughout Christendom.

Once the ceremonies were over, however, Charles passed decrees imposing a reign of terror upon Saxony. In previous years Charles' mother, Bertrada, and his old

NORSEMEN

CELTS

North Sea

DANES

Atlantic Ocean

ANGLO-
SAXONS

FRISIA

RHINE RIVER

Verden

SAXONY

ALLER RIVER

ODER RIVER

Paderborn

WESER RIVER

BRITTANY

Noyon

Aachen

AUSTRASIA

THURINGIA

UNSTRUT RIVER

SEINE

St. Denis

Paris

Soissons

Mainz

NEUSTRIA

RIVER

Worms

LOIRE RIVER

Tours

Auxerre

ALAMANNIA

DANUBE

FRANKISH KINGDOM

RIVER

AQUITAINE

BAVARIA

GASCONY

BURGUNDY

ALPS

GALICIA

PYRENEES

Roncesvalles

SPANISH MARCH

SEPTIMANIA

RHONE RIVER

Pavia

LOMBARDY

Venice

Ravenna

PAPAL

Adriatic Sea

EBRO RIVER

Saragossa

CALIPHATE

OF

CORDOBA

Barcelona

CORSICA

STATES

DUCHY
OF
SPOLETO

Rome

Cordoba

DUCHY
OF
BENEVENT

SARDINIA

Mediterranea

ARAB EMPIRE

CALA

SICILY

EUROPE c. 800

- Charles' Kingdom
- Carloman's Kingdom
- Conquests of Charlemagne
- Tributary to Charlemagne
- Allied to Charlemagne
- Byzantine Empire
- Arab Empire

altic Sea

S L A V I C

P E O P L E S

A V A R S

RIVER

DANUBE

PANNONIA

Black Sea

Constantinople

Nicaea

BYZANTINE EMPIRE

ARAB EMPIRE

Sea

Jerusalem

tutor, Abbot Fulrad, had repeatedly urged him to experiment with a policy of leniency in Saxony. But Fulrad as well as Bertrada had died recently, and there was no one to check the more savage side of Charles' nature, uppermost since the defeat at Roncesvalles. His decree on Saxony ordered the death penalty for any violation of Christian principles, for any offense against a priest or a church, and even for eating meat during Lent or cremating the dead in pagan fashion. To strengthen Saxon dependence on the Christian Church, Charles gave priests the power to absolve people guilty of crimes against Frankish law and to lift the death penalty after they had confessed. Churches were made places of refuge to which lawbreakers could flee for safety. In addition, the Saxons, already impoverished by years of war, were required to pay tithes to support the churches that Charles forced them to build. Finally, any commoner who killed his lord or lady was to be punished by death. By this clause in the Capitulary of Paderborn of 785, Charles was trying to protect the Saxon nobles who had supported him against the national uprising.

The Saxon people groaned under these additional burdens. They murmured against the total destruction of their traditional freedoms. But for the time being, they were too exhausted to make more than feeble protests. The harvest of hatred that Charles was sowing would take a while to sprout in the scorched earth of Saxony.

He was sowing hatred in his homeland as well, but even mild and humane advisors like Alcuin could no longer divert him from the course he had set. The brunt of the Saxon war had been borne by the Frankish lands east of the Rhine, especially Thuringia. The people resented the constant levies of men, the higher taxation, and the oppression of dishonest officials who profited by the king's preoccupation with graver matters. Poverty and famine spread as a direct result of Charles' war policies, and for the first time in Charles' reign a separatist movement took shape. Under the leadership of a Thuringian nobleman named Count Hardrad, the assassination of Charles—to be followed by a general rebellion—was plotted in the winter of 785–86.

Charles discovered the plot and moved swiftly. He invaded Thuringia as if it were a province of Saxony. His army, by now accustomed to looting and burning, devastated the land as if the rebellious peasants were a foreign foe. Count Hardrad and the other conspirators were seized; three were put to death, the others blinded or exiled. But punishment did not put an end to dissatisfaction, and

A vaguely Oriental-looking Charlemagne (above) addresses his second son, Pepin (opposite), in two details from a tenth-century manuscript made in Italy, where the young man ruled as king and tributary to his father. Both hold scepters denoting kingly status.

within a few years another and even more serious conspiracy came to a head.

This time no regional uprising was involved. Instead, a palace revolution was planned by men closely associated with the court. Charles himself, and his three sons by Hildigard—Charles, Carloman, and Louis—were to be assassinated and a figurehead was to be placed on the throne. The figurehead was to be none other than Pepin the Hunchback, Charles' son by his first wife, Himiltrude. This unfortunate boy had seen himself displaced by his half-brothers in his father's favor and in his prospects of succeeding to the throne. Even his name of Pepin had been given to one of these brothers, the one who formerly had been called Carloman. In solemn ceremony Pope Hadrian himself had at Charles' request rebaptized the boy Carloman as Pepin and crowned him King of Italy. At that same ceremony the youngest son, Louis, had been crowned King of Aquitaine. Only three years old, Louis had been dressed in miniature armor specially made for him, seated on a horse, and ridden into his kingdom. Presumably Charles was reserving the title of King of the Franks for his namesake son, young Charles, Hildigard's eldest. But for Pepin the Hunchback no provision at all had been made.

Under these circumstances, Pepin the Hunchback was easily persuaded to join the conspiracy against his father and brothers. The malcontent counts promised him the throne and succeeded in rallying around him and themselves all those who had reasons to oppose the King. The plot seems to have come within a hair of success; but at the last moment it was betrayed by a Lombard poet whom the conspirators had taken into their confidence. The poet, Fardulf, was rewarded by being appointed Abbot of St. Denis, near Paris, the great abbey where Charles' father and mother had been buried. Most of the conspirators were executed, and Pepin the Hunchback was actually condemned to death. Charles commuted this sentence, however, and the boy was confined to a monastery for life.

Charles had been profoundly shaken to find treason so close to home, in his own family and among noblemen whom he had thought his friends. Nevertheless, he continued for a time to pursue unwaveringly the policy of force that he had embarked on after the defeat at Roncesvalles. He used force at home to ensure loyalty; he used it on all his borders to enlarge his domains and create an empire.

One of the first great conquests of his middle years was bloodless. From the very beginning of his reign Charles had

Ci parle des eglises et des autres e
fices que lempereur edifia de ses femmes
et de ses enfans. Et comment ilz furent
nourris t entroduis Et puis parle dun
filz de bast qui auoit nom pepin. Et co
ment il fift conspiracion contre son pe
Et de la Vengeance des traiteurs.

been troubled by the ambiguous position of the great Duchy of Bavaria, ruled over by his cousin Tassilo. The Bavarians were Germans, like the Saxons and Lombards; and Charles' Anglo-Saxon advisors, such as Alcuin, had made him deeply aware of the essential linguistic and racial unity of the Germans. The very word for German—*diutisk*, from which the modern *deutsch* is derived—had been popularized by the Anglo-Saxon missionaries. Charles had become so interested in the concept of a German nation that he ordered some of his scholars to make a collection of the ancient German lays that preserved the acts and wars of the kings of old. He himself began writing a grammar of the German language, and he gave new names to the winds and the months, which previously had borne partly German and partly Latin names.

These cultural interests paralleled his political design to weld all the Germans on the Continent into a unified state. With the surrender of Widukind and the subsidence of resistance in Saxony, only the Bavarians remained outside his orbit. For twenty years Duke Tassilo of Bavaria had maneuvered skillfully to maintain his actual independence, while making gestures of nominal submission to Charles. Tassilo's wife, Liutperga, was one of the daughters of King Desiderius of Lombardy, whom Charles had deposed. One of her sisters was married to the Duke of Benevento, in southern Italy. Her brother Adelchis was an exile in Constantinople, forever trying to raise troops there so that he might return to Lombardy to recover his birthright. For years Liutperga had urged her husband to oppose Charles, and she had woven a network of intrigue among her relatives all over Europe in her efforts to thwart Charles' plans.

But Charles, too, had learned something about intrigue in these difficult years. By adroit diplomacy and a threat of force he secured the neutrality of the Duke of Benevento, over whose land he established a protectorate. Then, by making concessions to Pope Hadrian, he persuaded the Pope to threaten Duke Tassilo with anathema if the Duke failed to observe the oaths of submission he had sworn to Charles in years past. The papal reprimand helped to undermine Tassilo's power among his own people.

Saddened, Charlemagne orders the execution of traitors who had plotted to depose him. By the time the scene at left was painted, in the early fifteenth century, Charles was stylized as a white-bearded, patriarchal figure.

Charles' silver, and his promises to Bavarian nobles, weakened it still further.

When Charles had thus prepared the ground, he summoned Tassilo to attend a national assembly of the Franks at Worms. Not daring to put himself physically at the mercy of Charles, the Bavarian Duke refused to come, and thus Tassilo provided Charles with the desired pretext for declaring war. Charles mobilized one of the largest forces he had ever put into the field. Lombard troops advanced upon Bavaria from the south; Austrasian, Thuringian, and even Saxon contingents marched from the north and west; and Charles personally led still another army of his Latin-speaking subjects from the west. The purpose of this "innumerable host," as a contemporary called it, was to convince the Bavarians that resistance was hopeless.

Intimidated by the show of force, bribed by Charles' agents, fearing Pope Hadrian's anathema, the Bavarian nobles and clergy refused to support the Duke who had ruled them wisely for thirty years. Instead of answering his call to arms, they urged Tassilo to submit. Charles waited on the border while the Bavarian leaders negotiated with their Duke; and at last Tassilo yielded. In the fall of 787 he came before the king, placed his hands in those of Charles in token of homage, and gave Charles the staff of rule. Charles returned this symbol to him, whereupon Tassilo took the oath of allegiance: "O King, the world is given to you for the good of all, and I shall pay my due service to you forever."

Loaded with presents, as Widukind had been, Cousin Tassilo returned to Bavaria accompanied by Frankish commissioners, who took oaths of allegiance to Charles from every Bavarian. But the leniency Charles had shown to Tassilo was only a sham. The following summer, when Tassilo came to the national assembly, as he was now bound to do, he was promptly arrested. At an elaborately staged treason trial, Tassilo's own Bavarian subjects testified against him. Tassilo was accused of a variety of crimes: plotting to kill the Frankish *missi*, urging his subjects to swear false oaths of allegiance to Charles, conspiring with a foreign enemy. His accusers even raked up a charge that he had deserted the army of King Pepin

The copper-gilt and inlaid silver cup opposite bears the names of its owners, Duke Tassilo and his wife, Liutperga. The figure of Christ indicates its use as a communion chalice, although it also served as their wedding cup.

STIFTSBIBLIOTHEK ST. GALL: PHOTO ZUMBÜHL

A flag shaped like a fire-breathing dragon leads a company of lancers off to battle in this detail from the Psalter of Saint Gall, one of the richest Carolingian manuscripts, made between 872 and 920. Saint Gall, a town in northeastern Switzerland that grew up near a seventh-century abbey founded by an Irish missionary, was an important center of medieval learning.

twenty-five years earlier! The penalty for desertion was death, and the assembled Frankish nobles declared that Tassilo ought to be punished to the full extent of the law. But Charles consented to poor Tassilo's request that he be allowed to spend the rest of his life atoning for his sins as a monk. The former Duke was sent to the monastery of St. Goar; his sons, daughters, and wife were also confined to religious institutions for life.

The way was now clear for Charles to annex Bavaria to the Frankish kingdom, and he proceeded to do so with cold efficiency. The huge duchy was broken up into convenient administrative units. Many Bavarian nobles were sent into exile, and their places taken by Franks. Charles never hesitated to mix the populations of his multinational realm, in spite of his interest in national identities. He recognized national feelings as a source of weakness as well as of strength and made a point of sending Lombard counts to govern Aquitaine or Brittany, Thuringian nobles to Lombardy, and Aquitanian rulers to Bavaria or Saxony. The less his officials were identified with the lands they governed, the more capably they would rule in the King's name. By shifting them about, Charles kept them from turning their territories into private fiefs.

The annexation of Bavaria in 788 extended the territory under Charles' government an enormous distance to the east. Suddenly it brought him into direct contact with the Slavic peoples bordering the German lands. Mingling diplomacy with force, as he was now tending to do more and more, Charles allied himself with some of these tribes and made war on the most powerful of them, the Welatabians, whom the Franks called Wiltzi. With the great forces now at his disposal, he had little difficulty in establishing a protectorate over these Slavs. But aside from sending a few missionaries among them, he did not interfere with the tribal ways of the Slavs. Charles understood by now the limits of military power. He had no interest in trying to become an Alexander the Great. The Slavic lands in the east were organized as marches, buffer territories to protect Bavaria and Saxony, which were being incorporated into the Frankish kingdom as rapidly as possible.

The conquest of Bavaria also brought Charles into direct contact with another people who seemed strange and even exotic to the Franks. These were the Avars, a Mongolian folk who had arrived in Europe from Asia in the sixth century. They were a small, broad-shouldered people who seemed molded to their little ponies, like their cousins the Huns, with whom the Franks always confused them. In the first flush of their expansion the Avars had advanced all the way to the Oder River, then settled in the former breadbasket of the Roman Empire, Pannonia (which today is divided between Hungary and Yugoslavia). The emperors at Constantinople paid enormous subsidies to the Avars to keep the peace. At one time the emperors had given the khakhan (khan of khans), as the Avar ruler was called, as much as 120,000 gold pieces every year, as well as invaluable gifts of silks, spices, and even a golden bed. The treasures of two and a half centuries were locked up in the palace of the khakhan within the famous fortress known as the Ring, a great city or camp protected by no less than nine concentric walls.

The unfortunate Tassilo was charged with having been the immediate cause of war between the Frankish kingdom and the Avars. In a desperate attempt to preserve his free-

Young King Pepin's victory over the Avars is celebrated in a spirited manuscript painting. Charlemagne's son (left), riding over a felled opponent, lunges at the leader of the turbaned enemy host.

dom, it was said, he invited them to invade Lombardy and Bavaria. Whatever the truth of this accusation, in 788, the year that Tassilo was deposed, the Avars did launch an attack in force. They were repulsed, and afterward they sent ambassadors offering to make peace and to fix the borders between their own land and Bavaria and Lombardy. But Charles, for a variety of motives that included fear of Avar power, religious zeal to make converts, and the lure of the fabulous Avar treasures, resolved on war. In 791 he ordered his son Pepin, the young King of Italy, to march directly into Avar territory from Lombardy, while he himself levied troops from every part of his kingdom.

In his first trial at arms, Pepin was successful beyond expectations. Charles took pride in this son's exploits on the battlefield. He ordered three days of special thanksgiving prayers throughout his realm to celebrate Pepin's penetration of Avar country and his capture of one hundred fifty Avar prisoners, whom the young King let live "awaiting further orders from us." But the initial successes were deceptive, and many years of hard fighting remained. Charles himself, now in his fifties, did not take so great a personal part in this war as he would have done in the past. Moreover, he was busy elsewhere; there had been new uprisings in Saxony—uprisings that he punished by incessant campaigning and forced deportations. Thousands upon thousands of Saxons were removed from their homes and resettled in Frankish territory. The Avar war was conducted mainly by the team of capable generals whom Charles had meanwhile trained—the "paladins" of legend—such as Count William Toulouse, Count Gerold of Bavaria, Eric of Friuli, and Charles' own sons Charles and Pepin. His youngest son, Louis—who by a quirk of fate was to succeed him—was the one among his three sons by Hildigard who could not be relied on to command armies.

The Avar war reached its climax in 795, the fourth year of heavy fighting. Eric of Friuli broke through the famous Ring that surrounded the khakhan's palace and captured the great hoard. Fifteen wagonloads of gold coins, clasps, bracelets, jeweled swords, silver cups, silks, ivory carvings, and many other treasures were brought to the fine new palace that Charles was building at Aachen. The Franks stared in awe and delight as these riches were displayed. So much wealth entered the country all at once, while at the same time ordinary goods were scarce because of the war, that prices rose sharply. The great treasure proved a curse in disguise; Frankland suffered from severe inflation.

The following year an even greater victory by young Pepin added to the new wealth and worsened the inflation. Pepin, too, broke through the Avar Ring, found more of the immense treasure, and this time razed the Avar capital. Smaller campaigns followed in the succeeding years, until all of Pannonia was devastated and the independent political power of the Avars destroyed. Many of the Avars remained, of course, but as a people they disappeared from history so completely that "they vanished like the Avars" became a stock phrase in Eastern Europe. Charles' biographer, Einhard, wrote: "How many battles were fought there and how much blood shed can still be seen by the deserted condition of Pannonia. The place where the palace of the khakhan stood is so desolate that there is not so much as a trace of human habitation."

These victories brought about the submission of many of the lesser chiefs of the Avars. They agreed to accept Christianity, and some of them came to Charles' new capital at Aachen to be baptized. By this time Charles had passed through the period of darkness and harshness that had distorted his personality ever since the defeat at Roncesvalles. He now listened when such friends as Alcuin warned him that men could be forced to baptism but not forced to believe and that religious instruction should precede forced conversion. Alcuin reminded Charles of the mistakes that had been made in Saxony, where the people still paid only lip-service to Christianity. No tithes should be asked of the new converts, Alcuin argued. "Let those who have only just been won to the Faith be given—in the words of the Apostle Paul—milk, that is to say, gentle commandments," he wrote to Charles.

Charles incorporated these recommendations into his legislation for the newly conquered territory. For many years he had followed policies of sheer force, but now that he was past his fiftieth year he turned his energies more and more to peaceful pursuits and religious problems. Fighting continued on his borders, but the major wars were over. Part of the reason for this was his own mellowing temperament; but part of it was the new political situation. He had conquered all the lands that had formerly been buffers between Frankland and the two other great powers, the Byzantine Empire and the Arab Empire. Now the three great powers of the Mediterranean world were directly in contact with one another. Henceforth, war would mean war on a continental scale. Prudence and sanity called for a new era of diplomacy, not conflict.

A rare artifact of the Avars vanquished by Charles, this silver-plated bronze bracelet of the eighth century was found in Hungary.

KING'S COURT AND GOD'S CITY

The last decade of the eighth century was the great era of building and intellectual development in the life of Charles the Great. Those years were presided over by a new wife, Charles' fifth, Liutgard. Fastrada had died in 794, and Charles never liked to remain long unmarried. Liutgard, beautiful and cultured, was loved all the more by the court because Fastrada had been so thoroughly disliked. Bishop Theodulf of Orléans describes Liutgard as a member of the Palace Academy: "Generous of hand, gentle of soul and mild of speech, doing good to all and working harm to none, she studiously pursues the liberal arts."

Liutgard was fortunate in that, unlike Charles' earlier wives, she had a permanent household. The growing bureaucracy of a far-flung empire had made a capital city a necessity. It was impossible to govern so vast a territory with all the records of administration being bundled from place to place in oxcarts or stored in a dozen different locations. Moreover, Charles himself had by now become so ardent in the pursuit of learning that he begrudged the time wasted in endless travel from palace to palace. Thus, in 794 he established as his capital Aachen (or Aix-la-Chapelle, as the French call it), situated in the rolling hill country between the Rhine and the Meuse rivers. This was a region that for centuries had been the heart of his family's power.

Aachen had been famous for its medicinal waters since the time of the Romans, but it had remained a small town until Charles made it his capital. The new capital was strategically located for governing the northern and north-

By the fourteenth century, Charlemagne was being venerated as a saint, and bones from his body—first exhumed in 1000—were placed in jewel-studded reliquaries like the one at left holding his leg bones. Flanked by two clerics, Charles holds his Aachen church, a door ornament of which appears above.

western part of Charles' domain, and the nearby Rhine River provided a great artery to the south. To facilitate rapid transport back and forth between the capital at Aachen and the Avar lands to the east, then under attack, Charles even attempted to dig a Rhine-Danube canal. He employed thousands of men to construct a huge ditch, more than a mile long and three hundred feet wide, which was intended to connect two small tributaries of the Rhine and the Danube. But bad weather ruined much of the work; heavy rains repeatedly washed mud back into the ditch; and the undertaking was soon abandoned. In fact, the project was too ambitious for the limited technology of the age; not until the middle of the nineteenth century was a Rhine-Danube canal successfully engineered.

Although the canal was a failure, Charles' other major building projects succeeded. At Mainz he had a great wooden bridge erected over the Rhine, so that the river need no longer be crossed by ferries or by bridges of boats. At Aachen itself he employed much of the gold captured from the Avars to create the magnificent palace and chapel that his contemporaries regarded as wonders of the world. Set atop a small hill, the palace was crowned by a bronze eagle with outstretched wings. The reception hall alone was one hundred fifty feet long by sixty-five feet wide. A whole complex of attached buildings contained such amenities as a library, a weapons room, and a marble swimming pool fed by hot springs and large enough for a hundred persons to bathe in at one time. Charles himself was exceedingly fond of swimming. He was said to surpass all others at his court in skill at this sport.

From the palace a long gallery, covered to provide protection from snow and rain, led down the hill to the wonderful octagonal chapel—"half human, half divine"—built by Odo of Metz. The original chapel still stands, much as it was in Charles' day, although a whole cathedral was erected around it in later centuries. Charles spared no expense in the adornment of his church. The cupola was roofed in lead and topped by a golden pine cone; the doors were made of solid bronze. With advancing years Charles grew increasingly pious and used to attend services at the chapel three or four times a day. Carved out of a single stone, the throne in which he sat during Mass may still be seen in the gallery of the cathedral at Aachen.

Town and palace swarmed with a gay, colorful, busy throng. Many officials were attached to the court, and the more important of them built their homes around the palace itself. By the middle of the last decade of the century Charles had been reigning for nearly thirty years. Time, along with the increase in his domain, had produced a vast expansion of the bureaucracy needed to rule. In addition to managing the affairs of the Church, the King's chaplain was in charge of the archives and the scribes—a function that he partly shared with the chancellor. In turn, the chancellor also advised the King on matters of foreign policy. The count of the palace combined the offices of justice of a supreme court and secretary of the interior. The chamberlain was the treasurer for both the King's household and the finances of the country as a whole—no attempt was made to keep these accounts separate. The constable managed the royal stables and appears also to have had the cavalry under his command. The chief doorkeeper was the equivalent of a modern appointments secretary; he determined who would be admitted to see the King. All these officials had sizable staffs and many servants working under them. In modern terms, they were the heads of departments of the government.

BIBLIOTHEQUE MUNICIPALE, TOULOUSE: PHOTO YAN

BILDARCHIV FOTO MARBURG

Later additions to the Aachen cathedral surround Charlemagne's octagonal chapel (center dome in photograph at left). Begun in 796, this finest example of Carolingian architecture was rebuilt in 983. Above, Charles supervises construction.

AACHEN MONUMENT

Charles, according to Einhard, "was a constant worshiper" at the octagonal chapel (left) that is the glory of Aachen Cathedral; during services he loved to sing but only "in low tone, and with others." The Emperor was especially proud of his chapel's radical design, a lofty vaulted octagon encircled by an ambulatory with open galleries above. Focal point of the galleries today is the simple but impressive marble throne (right) from which Charles could look down and across to the altar.

Stirred by visions of ancient glory, the Saxon Holy Roman Emperor Otto III opened the Aachen tomb of his illustrious predecessor Charlemagne in the year 1000. After Charles' subsequent beatification, his bones were distributed among reliquaries. The silver-gilt leg reliquary below (also shown on page 84) is decorated with high-relief portraits of succeeding emperors. The panels at top (see pages 53, 104–05, 140–41) depict scenes from his life.

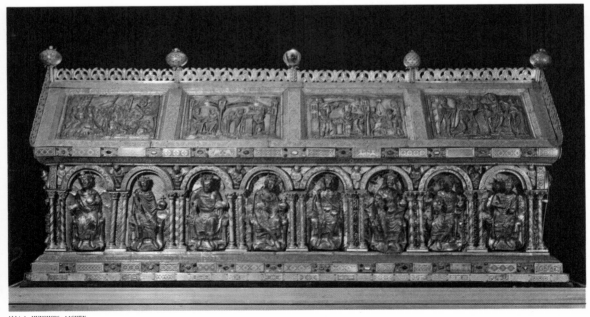

There was a great deal of routine work to be got through, and Charles made the most of every minute. Even while he was dressing in the mornings, he had officials, petitioners, and contestants in lawsuits admitted to his antechamber. Not that his dressing was a prolonged affair, for he preferred the simple linen clothes that his subjects wore. He used to reprove his more foppish underlings for indulging themselves in expensive Oriental silks. But although he preferred plain garments on himself, he liked to see his beautiful wife, Liutgard, wearing jeweled collars. Even his horse was decked out with gold and silver.

Charles also indulged his daughters. Indeed, he loved them so dearly that he would never allow them to marry away from home—even when the Byzantine Emperor bid for the hand of one. The poet Angilbert, who married Princess Bertha, has described Charles' daughters attending a hunt. There was Rotrud, "her pale blonde hair intertwined with ribbons of violet and strings of pearls, a coronet of gold circling her head." After her came Bertha, Angilbert's wife, "wearing a golden diadem, with golden filaments sparkling in her gleaming hair, her snowy shoulders covered by an ermine wrap, her belt shining in many colors." Then "lily-white Gisla, appareled in a purple gown shot through with tints of mauve, her face, her hair gleaming with many lights." Next came Rothaid: "On her breast, on her throat, among her hair flash jewels of various sorts. A silk mantle drapes her white shoulders. Above her radiant forehead a coronet of pearls gleams. A gold pin mounted with a pearl crowns her coiffure." Even Theotrade, who was a teen-ager at the time this poem was written, wore "rare emeralds adorning her lovely neck."

Angilbert goes on to describe the hunt itself:

A wild boar dashes across the valley, the hounds in hot pursuit. . . . The forest rings with the loud echoes of the wild din. The notes of the horn rouse and quicken the most savage instincts of the savage brutes and lead them to where the infuriated boar shows its terrible tusks.

The rustling leaves drop from the shaken boughs; the boar escapes, bounds away from its pursuers up the steepest places. Grunting fiercely, it climbs the most inaccessible points of the

The exciting climax of a hunt was captured by a fourteenth-century French artist, who depicted hunters and hound (opposite, above) in close pursuit of a stag. The elephant-tusk hunting horn below (similar to the one in use above) was long known as Charlemagne's, although it was made in Italy two centuries after his death. Animals and arabesques decorate it.

BIBLIOTHÈQUE NATIONALE, SERVICE PHOTOGRAPHIQUE: MSS. FR. NOUVELLES ACQUISITIONS 1098 FOL. 50

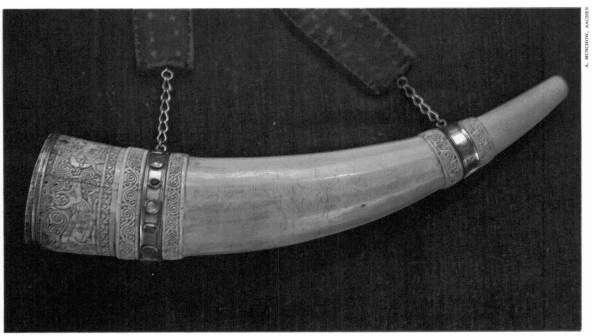

A. MÜNCHOW, AACHEN

rocky crest. At last, exhausted by its efforts and unable to run any longer, it sits panting on its haunches. The dogs have tasted its blood and felt its tusk. Some are driven back; others, fiercer than the rest, are tossed bleeding into the air.

At that supreme moment the King arrives on the scene. Fleeter than the bird in its flight, he breaks through the crowd, strikes the beast's breast with his sword, and drives the cold blade home to the hilt. The wild boar falls, blood streaming from the deadly wound, and dies. . . . The whole royal family, girls and all, have witnessed the feat from a commanding point.

It was a cruel sport, but all the men of the Middle Ages shared Charles' passion for hunting. And the sport had at least the justification that it provided meat for the royal tables. When Charles sat down to dinner, the main course would be a roast of the game that had been killed during the morning hunt. During the meal, one of the poets of the household, Alcuin or Theodulf or Angilbert, might rise to read aloud a poem—much to the dismay of the simple men-at-arms, who sometimes clapped their hands to their heads and glared at the poet until Charles reproved them. Contrary to the practice in the halls of most nobles, there was little heavy drinking at dinner. Charles "despised drunkenness in everyone, and especially in himself and his

A meeting of Church elders is depicted in this pen drawing from the famed Utrecht Psalter, made about 832 when the memory of Charles' councils was fresh. At center, two versions of the sacred texts on lecterns are compared.

friends." He preferred, as Alcuin put it, "the wine of learning." If there were no poems offered, Charles would frequently follow the monastic practice of having someone read aloud at dinner from histories or from his favorite book, St. Augustine's *The City of God.*

St. Augustine is not an easy writer to understand. His theological subtleties have provided food for discussion for fifteen hundred years. But Charles, warrior, hunter, and ruler though he was primarily, also took a deep interest in theological questions. He was actively involved in the two chief doctrinal struggles of his time: the question of the nature of Christ and the movement known as iconoclasm, or "image-breaking." These two theological controversies entered Frankland from Spain and from Constantinople respectively, both places where Christianity came into contact with the skepticism of the Moslem world.

The question of the nature of Christ led to the heresy known as adoptionism. From the very beginnings of Christianity the problem of how Christ could be at once man and God, both a human being and the divine Ruler of the universe, had agitated philosophers and theologians and even the laity. It was hard to imagine how God could perform the ordinary human acts of sleeping, eating, and drinking, let alone suffering pain and dying. Many solutions were proposed, and almost every one gave rise to a new heresy or a new orthodoxy.

Adoptianism arose in Spain, where first Bishop Elipand of Toledo and then Bishop Felix of Urgel declared that Christ, when a man, could not possibly have been the true son of God but must have been an adopted son. Felix had a reputation for saintliness, and his opinion carried along a large part of the Spanish Church. Even though Pope Hadrian soon condemned it, the doctrine spread so rapidly through Spain and Aquitaine that, before long, in the words of a contemporary, there were "two churches quarreling with each other over the One Christ."

Charles took alarm. In Frankland, Church and State were so closely interrelated that schism in the Church seriously endangered the internal peace of the State. Moreover, the people at large in his dominions took a passionate interest in such questions, as did Charles himself. Religious disagreements in his day were as divisive as ideological disputes are today. The king therefore resolved to check the spreading heresy, and to that end he called a council of his bishops to meet at Regensburg, there to discuss adoptionism. Bishop Felix of Urgel was ordered to attend.

An incident of the iconoclast controversy appears in a 1066 Greek Psalter made at Constantinople. Two saints (left, above) bear an icon to the Byzantine Emperor (below), who orders retainers to obliterate the image with lime.

With Charles himself presiding over the discussions, and making his own orthodox opinions clear from the start, the decisions of the council were a foregone conclusion. Bishop Felix recanted. After a brief sojourn in Italy—where Pope Hadrian sentenced him to compose a treatise exposing the *errors* of adoptionism—the unhappy bishop returned to Spain. There he immediately resumed his fight for his beliefs. The heresy continued to win followers, and in 794 Charles convened another council, this time at Frankfurt, to debate the question once more. He himself addressed this council. It is recorded that he spoke "long and fluently" and formulated the orthodox opinion in the words: "The Son of God became the Son of Man and by virtue of his divine nature was born the Son of God, by virtue of his human nature the Son of Man." Thus he was "both true God and true Man."

Bishop Felix and the Spanish bishops had not attended this council. But they sent a lengthy treatise, full of quotations from the Fathers of the Church. Some of their arguments were so perplexing or persuasive that the churchmen at the council took several days to discuss the issue—in spite of Charles' forthright declaration that "it is necessary to exterminate this insane pestilence by the use of every means." But at last the council condemned the Felician heresy, and Charles issued a warning to the Spanish bishops that he would abandon the Spanish March to the Saracens unless they returned "to the arms of your tender mother, the Church."

Several years passed before Bishop Felix and his chief supporters among the Spanish and Aquitanian bishops, under unrelenting pressure from King and Pope, once more recanted. The adoptionist heresy was finally suppressed, formally, but for centuries it never really died out entirely in southern France and northern Spain. Its doctrines prepared the soil for the great heresy known as Catharism, which sprang up in those regions during the twelfth century only to be drowned in blood by the Albigensian Crusaders in the thirteenth century.

Long before the Frankfurt council Charles and his bishops had devoted much of their time to considering the other great religious question of the age: the proper attitude of a Christian toward images. The Judaic, Old Testament prohibition "Thou shalt make no graven images" had been adopted by the early Christian Church. But gradually the custom had developed of adorning churches with images of Christ, the Virgin, and the saints and with pic-

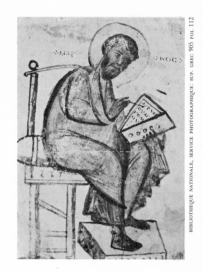

St. Mark, at work composing his Gospel, is seen in this eighth-century detail, a rare sample of pre-iconoclast Byzantine painting.

OVERLEAF: *Among the finest examples of Byzantine art still in existence are the sixth-century mosaics at Ravenna, the Adriatic city captured in 756 by Charles' father and donated to the popes. Frankish warriors, pausing there, would scarcely have guessed that their King's son would come to rival the Eastern Roman Emperor, here represented by Justinian, accompanied by armed attendants and clerics bearing ritualistic offerings.*

torial narratives of Bible stories. As early as the fourth and fifth centuries some bishops and theologians objected to pictures on the grounds that they "defiled the church." But Pope Gregory the Great gave religious images his sanction. In a letter to the Bishop of Marseilles, who had ordered all images removed from his church, Pope Gregory wrote: "We altogether praise you for forbidding adoration of the pictures, but we blame you for having destroyed them. . . . To adore a picture is a different matter from learning about the object of adoration through the story that the picture tells." Pictures on the walls of churches were a necessity, Gregory declared, in order that the illiterate people could at least learn some of the history of their faith from the stories depicted in paint and stone.

Gregory's view was on the whole accepted by the Western Church. But in the East the influence of Islam and Judaism was strong; and both these religions prohibited images. "Statues are an abomination of Satan's work," says the Koran, thus paralleling the Old Testament commandment. In the East, moreover, the adoration of images had taken far more intense forms than in the West. Icons (from the Greek word for "pictures") were to be found in every home as well as in every church; and many of them were believed to be of miraculous origin. The common people and the monks tended to worship them as in the past they had worshiped pagan idols. Therefore the reaction against images among conscientious and scrupulous men of religion was all the stronger.

Early in the eighth century the Byzantine Emperor Leo the Isaurian employed the power of the State to combat what he regarded as the superstitious adoration of images. For half a century the Eastern Empire was racked by the struggle between iconoclasts and iconodules, image-smashers and image-worshipers. Leo's attacks on images aroused the hostility of the monks and the women of the empire in particular. His successor, Constantine V, met the opposition to iconoclasm head on by persecuting the monks and closing monasteries. In the West, meanwhile, the popes denounced the whole movement as outright heresy. Western hostility toward iconoclasm marked the beginning of an ultimately unhealable breach between the Eastern and the Western churches. It was also one of the factors that prompted the popes to turn to the Franks, and away from the Byzantine Empire, for secular support.

With the accession to the throne of the Eastern Empire of Constantine VI in 780, the first period of intense icono-

Charles' veneration of religious relics—as opposed to the image worship into which he feared the Eastern Church was slipping—is shown in this scene of the King and another royal figure kneeling before the relic being carried aloft by two passing priests.

clasm came to an end. Constantine's mother, Irene, who ruled as regent for her minor son, reversed the policy of her predecessors and restored image worship. In 787 she called a great council of the Church at Nicaea to provide the iconodule party with the organization and the theological support it had hitherto lacked. The council's decrees confirmed veneration of holy images and called for restoration of paintings, statues, and mosaics that the zealots of the reforming iconoclasts had removed from Eastern churches.

Pope Hadrian had sent observers to this council, and he did not contest its claim to being the Seventh Ecumenical Council, that is, a council of the entire Church. Pleased that the heretical iconoclastic movement in the East had been crushed, he accepted the decrees of the council. But he delayed sending his official approval because he wanted Empress Irene to return to the papacy those estates in her territory that had been confiscated by earlier iconoclastic emperors.

In the meantime Hadrian sent Charles a Latin translation of the Nicaean decrees. Charles was shocked; it seemed to him that the "Greeks," as he called them, had fallen from one heresy into another at the opposite extreme, that they were lapsing into the basest sort of pagan idolatry. He and all the thinkers of his Palace Academy began studying the Fathers of the Church and discussing the theological problems involved. They came up with a list of eighty-five criticisms of the Council of Nicaea. Charles ordered his son-in-law Angilbert to deliver this list to Pope Hadrian for comment.

The Pope was acutely embarrassed by what he regarded as Charles' amateur theologizing. He could not very well accuse the King, his friend and protector, of heresy; but he could bring himself to accept only one of the eighty-five theses, the one in which Charles had written (in the spirit of Pope Gregory the Great): "We permit anyone who wishes, for the love of God and his saints, to set up images inside or outside the churches, but we shall never force anyone to worship them, nor allow any others to destroy them." This was clearly a statement of the moderate viewpoint to which most theologians of the Western Church subscribed.

Charles was angered by the Pope's rejection of his views. Like the Byzantine emperors themselves, Charles considered himself the governor as well as the defender of the Church, a priest-king whose anointment had made him sacred. Ultimately, in his view, even popes must take orders

Three eighth-century coins are decorated with highly stylized portraits of Byzantium's royalty. At the top is Emperor Leo III, an iconoclast. Below are his successor Constantine V and Constantine's mother, Irene, an iconodule.

Frequent heresies plagued Christianity's early centuries, and in summoning the Second Council of Nicaea to deal with iconoclasm, Irene was following the precedent of earlier emperors. At right is a miniature from a book of Church festivals made for one of Irene's successors, Basil II (963–1025). The scene, of a groveling heretic recanting his unorthodox beliefs before a group of stern Church fathers, is supposed to represent an incident of the Nicaean council. The beardless figure (fourth from left) may be Irene's son, the boy Emperor Constantine VI.

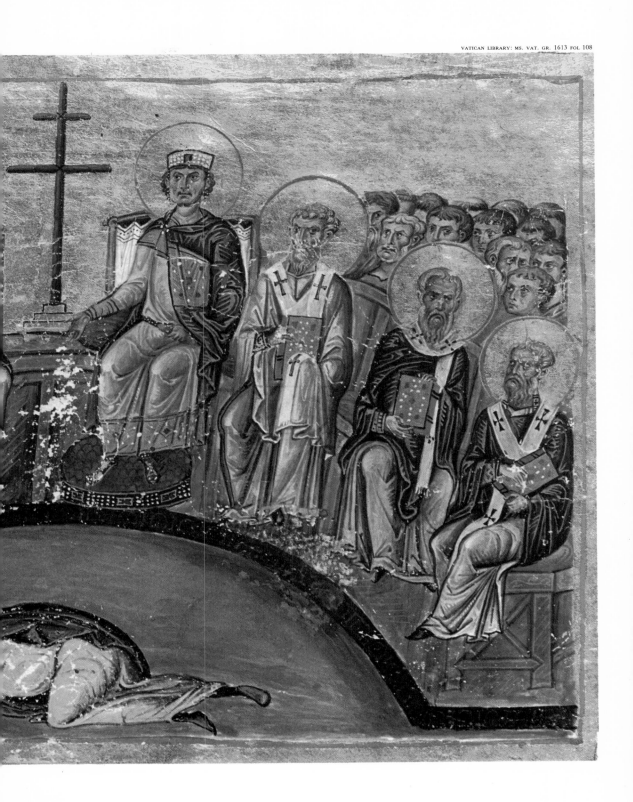

from divinely appointed rulers. He therefore initiated work on the long tract that bears his name, the *Caroline Books*, in which the whole subject of image worship was thrashed out. Undoubtedly Charles was aided in the writing by his literary friends, such as Alcuin and Bishop Theodulf of Orléans; but the angry tone and political references of the treatise suggest that Charles himself inspired a large part of it.

The *Caroline Books* were presented to the Frankfurt council of 794 as the opinion of Frankland on the subject of image worship. The papal legates present voted along with the bishops of Frankland to condemn the doctrines of the Council of Nicaea and to deny its claim that it was ecumenical. The Nicene Council by no means represented the whole Church, they insisted. Pope Hadrian could not bring himself to ratify this assertion, but he also did not dare to object. He was far too dependent on Charles to risk offending him twice. Moreover, Hadrian was an old man, and ill. Shortly afterward, on Christmas Day, 795, he died.

It is recorded that Charles wept on hearing of Hadrian's death. In spite of their disagreements over doctrines, not to mention territory, Charles felt as if he had lost a member of his family. He ordered prayers for Hadrian throughout his lands, provided a marble stone for Hadrian's tomb, and had an epitaph written by Alcuin inscribed on the tombstone in letters of gold. For twenty years Hadrian had labored with him to weld the nations of western Europe into something approaching that *City of God* of which St. Augustine wrote. Together, they had reformed the liturgy of the Church in Frankland, making it conform to the Roman liturgy. Together, they had sought to oppose the secularization of the clergy, to prevent bishops and abbots from hunting and hawking, churchmen from bearing arms, monks and nuns from wandering idly about the countryside. Charles had frequently consulted Hadrian on questions of ecclesiastical law. He had made an attempt to enforce the principles and practices set forth in the canons of the Church.

Now Hadrian was dead, and Charles would miss him. It is easy to believe that Charles actually wept, for this man of iron also had the gift of tears, as it was called in his day —his contemporaries believed that to be able to weep easily was a special blessing conferred by God. But his sadness turned to alarm when news came across the Alps of the man who had so quickly been elected Supreme Pontiff to succeed his old friend Hadrian.

Pope Hadrian, Charles' longtime friend, appears on a broken coin.

Charles' lifelong devotion to Christianity and patronage of the Church is symbolized in this tableau from the fourteenth-century Grandes Chroniques de France. *A kneeling bishop presents to Charles a model church—its key prominently showing—perhaps one of the many he endowed.*

OVERLEAF: *In a panel from Charles' reliquary, the King kneels before the Virgin and Child, offering a model of his Aachen church. Flanking the trio are a bishop (left) and an angel.*

103

Si comence le second liure des hystoires cha
lemaine, premierement coment il fut cou
ronne a empereur en leglise saint pierre
de romme. Apres coment il condampna
par cil ceulx qui auoient laidi lapostol
lyon. Et puis des troulles des terres qui
furent par le monde, & des messaiges & pri
aaron le roy de perse se
i roux de la natiuite en
tra lempereur en leglise
saint pierre de romme
droit en ce point que on

VI

CHARLES AUGUSTUS

The new Pope, Leo III, had been unanimously elected on December 26, 795, the very day of Hadrian's funeral. But Leo evidently had a bad reputation among those Franks who knew something about the internal politics of the papal court at Rome. The exact nature of the charges against him has been veiled by the discretion of the contemporary writers; Alcuin, for example, hastily burned a letter from the Bishop of Salzburg because it gave some details. The good-hearted and pious Alcuin feared that the letter might stir still more gossip if it fell into the wrong hands. Nevertheless, there are enough hints in the messages of Charles to the Pope, and in some other sources, to suggest that the new Supreme Pontiff may not have been "a shining example of perfect holiness," as Charles recommended that he ought to be.

Given the situation in Rome, there is nothing surprising about that. Although Leo himself may have been of humble origin, most popes were members of the Roman nobility; papal elections were usually influenced by hostile factions among the great families of Rome. It was always possible for a man of less than saintly character to ascend to the Chair of St. Peter. To the Romans—who had popes among them all the time—the person of a pope was not particularly sacred.

Even after papal elections, factionalism could and did continue. Rome had long been a hotbed of conspiracy, but under Leo III the intrigues seem to have been more virulent than usual. In April of 799 two of the highest papal officials, Paschalis and Campulus—one the nephew of Hadrian, the other the late Pope's secretary, and both his

At left, Pope Leo crowns Charles Holy Roman Emperor in St. Peter's Basilica on Christmas Day, 800. The fifteenth-century French court painter Jean Fouquet added imperial eagles to fleurs-de-lis on the tall standards. The tapestry detail above shows Charlemagne as founder of a diocese in Saxony.

107

possible successors—conspired to maim and unseat Leo. A gang of their followers ambushed the Pope as he was riding in a procession. The Pope was pulled from his horse, stripped of his robes, and given a frightful beating. Then he was hauled away as a prisoner and held in the monastery of St. Erasmus. He afterward alleged that the conspirators had attempted to blind him and to cut out his tongue.

Fortunately, the papal chamberlain found out where the Pope was being held. Under cover of night he slipped into the monastery with a rope and lowered Leo down the walls. Leo escaped to St. Peter's, which then lay outside Rome proper. By that time, rioting had broken out in the city; opponents and followers of the Pope fought each other in the streets. Charles' Frankish vassal in Spoleto, Duke Winigis, had to rush to Rome with troops to rescue Pope Leo and restore order. Winigis then sent word to Charles of what had happened. The King, exercising the rights that he held as Patrician of the Romans and ruler of most of

A graphic depiction of the attempted blinding of Leo III appears in the Chronique du Monde, *a fourteenth-century world history. As two conspirators attack the prostrate Pope, another restrains his clerical attendants.*

Italy, commanded Winigis to send the Pope to him at his camp in Paderborn, Saxony.

No one questioned his right to issue such an order. For by this last year of the eighth century, Charles had been ruling for thirty years, and it had come to be a matter of course for his people to refer to him as Charles the Great—Carolus Magnus, Karl der Grosse, Charlemagne. The intellectuals of his court, the intimates of his Palace Academy, who joked and exchanged poems and riddles with him, were themselves awed by the greatness of their King. He who had inherited only half a realm in Frankland now ruled from the shores of the Atlantic to the forests of Bohemia, from the Spanish March south of the Pyrenees to beyond the mouth of the Elbe, from Calabria in the toe of Italy's boot to the border of Denmark, from the source of the Rhine in Switzerland to its estuary in the Netherlands, and from the source of the Danube in the Black Forest to what is now Belgrade, Yugoslavia. (See map, pages 72–73.)

An undersized Charles kneels to receive the blessing of Pope Leo, grateful for the Frankish King's support following the conspiracy. The North German history from which this scene also comes focuses on events at Rome.

From all these lands vast revenues as well as the spoils of war poured into the King's coffers.

But material possessions were not the sole reason for Charlemagne's present greatness. Even while his armies marched everywhere in Europe, he had cultivated the things of the spirit and the arts of peace. He had built schools, reformed the Church, and given to his people a new system of weights and measures and a new coinage, a new attitude toward learning, and a new cosmopolitanism in the arts. Even in matters of religion Charles seemed greater than the Pope, for he had taken the lead in combating heresies. Alcuin, the most learned man of his age, could call the King "illumined with the light of all knowledge," so wise that he could see through "all that is mystery and darkness, down to the very bottom of things." That sounds like a courtier's flattery; but Alcuin was a man of clear, simple-hearted integrity who meant what he said.

Alcuin was also deeply orthodox. To his mind, the Pope could do no wrong because he was the Pope. The charges Alcuin had heard—that Leo was guilty of "adultery and perjury"—must be false; Alcuin saw no other possibility. And Alcuin, whose opinion was highly respected by Charles, urged the King to support the Pope and punish the conspirators. In his letter to Charles, Alcuin stated simply what he believed intensely: that the weight of the whole world rested on Charles' shoulders.

Hitherto there have been three persons in the highest position in the world. The first was that Apostolic Sublimity who rules as Vicar in the Chair of Saint Peter, and you have informed me of what has been done to him. The second is the imperial dignity and secular power of the Second Rome [Constantinople], and everyone is talking about how impiously its emperor has been deposed, not by foreigners, but by his own fellow citizens. The third is the royal dignity in which you have been placed by the dispensation of our Lord Jesus Christ, so that you are ruler of the Christian people. Your power is more excellent than theirs, your wisdom more shining, your royal dignity more sublime. Behold, upon you alone rests the salvation of the churches of Christ.

The events in Constantinople to which Alcuin referred in this letter had shocked the Western World even more than the attack upon Pope Leo. The Empress Irene, who had been regent from 780 to 790, during the minority of her son, Constantine VI, had temporarily yielded the throne to him when he came of age. Thereafter she pursued a deliberate policy of cultivating his vices and undermining his popularity, and at last she organized a conspiracy against

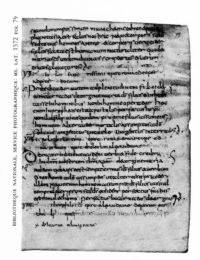

A Latin version of decisions made at an early Church council contains marginal notes by Alcuin, always interested—as was Charles—in the fine points of Church doctrine.

Classical texts were studied at Charles' court. A tenth-century copy of a Latin allegory first compiled five centuries earlier shows Grammar, first of the seven liberal arts, presiding at the wedding of Eloquence and Learning.

Arms entwined on a single throne, king and pope are pictured in an idealized relationship. The ruler's sword protects the churchman, whose crosier, or pastoral staff, symbolizes rule over his spiritual flock. Charles' support of the papacy was an exception to the usual rivalry of Church and State.

An eclipse of the sun supposedly greeted Irene's cruel order to depose and blind her son, Constantine VI. The artist of the fourteenth-century Chronique du Monde *visualized the event's effect on voyagers at sea (below). Reappearing, an angry sun terrifies sailors in storm-tossed vessels.*

him. In 797 her henchmen seized the unfortunate young man and had his eyes put out. Irene thereupon declared herself Emperor—rather than Empress.

To Charles and his court and to other thinking men in the West, this claim was absurd. How could a woman, and moreover a criminal and a cruel mother, be the Roman Emperor? Rather, the throne of the Roman Empire was vacant; that was self-evident, and the question now arose of who ought to be seated on it. To ask this question was to answer it: there was only one candidate.

Such were the thoughts that stirred Charles and his advisors as they made their preparations for the reception of Pope Leo at Paderborn in the summer of 799. For all that Leo was charged with grave crimes, he was still the supreme head of Christendom, and Charles was determined to show him all due respect. Remembering that forty-six years earlier he himself had been sent by his own father to greet Pope Stephen, Charles sent his twenty-two-year-old son, King Pepin of Italy, to salute Leo. With the blasts of trumpets, the clangor of clashing shields and spears, an army, which only a short time before had been forcibly removing unhappy Saxons from their homes, greeted the Pope. Young Pepin guided the Pope between lanes of soldiers to where Charles stood in the center of a circle of warriors and clergy, his armor shining like silver, a golden helmet on his head. Charles came forward, knelt for the Pope's blessing, then rose to embrace him. Hand in hand they entered the church, where the Pope celebrated a pontifical Mass. This was followed by a banquet at which Falernian wine was served in golden goblets.

The writers of the age were given to describing elaborately the outward circumstances of meetings between great personages but telling little of what was said or what decisions were reached. Thus one is compelled to judge the subject of the discussions only by what happened thereafter, and doubt will always remain whether the subsequent events were planned in detail at Paderborn, or whether some matters were left to chance. It can scarcely be doubted that a great deal was planned. Apparently Charles accepted Pope Leo's explanations of his difficulties and agreed to restore the Pope to power in Rome. To that end, in October, Charles sent the Pope back to Italy, escorted by the archbishops of Salzburg and Cologne and by a large detachment of Frankish troops.

Back in Rome at the end of the year 799, the Frankish archbishops and other dignitaries heard the testimony of

113

the conspirators, who attempted to justify their attack on the Pope by presenting evidence against him. However, the evidence was adjudged insufficient, and the accusers were sent to Frankland to be dealt with by Charles himself.

In March of the year 800, Charles began a great progress around his dominions to put everything in order before he visited Rome again, as he had decided to do. He went to the English Channel coast of France and ordered the erection of watchtowers to guard against the Vikings, who were just beginning the raids that would become so terrible a plague in the next century. At Tours he met his son Louis and inquired into the affairs of Aquitaine. Here, too, he had many conferences with the aging Alcuin, now Abbot of Tours. And at Tours the last of his five wives, the lovely Liutgard, suddenly died, and Charles mourned her bitterly. But even this blow of fate could not deter him from the grandiose project he had in mind. He traversed nearly the whole of Frankland, from the Loire Valley back to Mainz on the Rhine, where the national assembly of the Franks was held in August. There he announced to his followers that he intended to visit Italy, to regulate the affairs of the papacy and of his Lombard kingdom. With a large army and many wagonloads of silver and gold ornaments that he intended to present to the churches of the Eternal City, Charlemagne set out once more for Rome.

Arriving in Rome a month before Christmas, he found the Roman nobility and populace cowed but still grumbling at the restoration of Pope Leo to office. The streets rang with gossip about the Pope's alleged sins or crimes. Obviously, something had to be done to clear Leo's name; and Charles could think of no way but a public trial, shocking though that was. He convoked a council of churchmen and nobles to investigate the charges against Leo and ordered the conspirators brought back from Frankland to Rome to testify.

The annals of the time do not give us details of the trial. But it went on for three weeks and ended in a "hung jury": the council could not decide for or against Pope Leo. At last a solution to this embarrassment was found: Pope Leo agreed to purge himself by oath. Such oaths, invoking God, the Apostles, and the saints, accorded with the legal ideas of the age, although it was usual for the accused to have "compurgators"—that is, persons who would swear along with him that he was not guilty. But since there was no precedent for a Pope's swearing, there was also no precedent for compurgation in the case of the Supreme Pontiff.

Whose word, after all, could carry more weight than that of the Pope himself? On December 23, therefore, Pope Leo swore alone: "I have not committed or caused to be committed the heinous crimes of which I have been accused." Then everyone sang the hymn *Te Deum laudamus* ("We praise Thee, O God"), and the case was considered closed.

Two days later, on Christmas Day, A.D. 800, Romans, Franks, Bavarians, Lombards, Goths, Basques, and even visiting Anglo-Saxons and Greeks crowded into St. Peter's Basilica, filling its great central nave and four huge aisles. Close to the altar were the King's daughters, two of his sons, Charles and Pepin, and Charles himself, dressed in a long Roman tunic and cloak, with a golden belt and jeweled sandals. During the Mass, Pope Leo suddenly lifted from the altar a golden crown, stepped forward, and as Charles rose from kneeling, placed the crown on the head of the King. The Basilica shook with the roar of the crowd: "Long life and victory to Charles Augustus, crowned by God the great and pacific Emperor of the Romans." Three times, in keeping with the ancient custom, the people hailed Charles as Emperor and Augustus.

Then Pope Leo prostrated himself before Charles and kissed the hem of his cloak in Byzantine fashion.

That act, acclamation by the Roman people, was the proper legal form for proclaiming an emperor. Charles had become Emperor of the West, the first since A.D. 476. The Roman Empire in the West had been revived and was to live on for another thousand years, in plenitude of power through the medieval centuries and as a shadowy ghost by the time Napoleon Bonaparte forced the abdication of the last Holy Roman Emperor, Francis II, in 1806.

There is a mystery and a controversy about this coronation. Indeed, the riddle has not been fully solved in the more than eleven and a half centuries that have passed since that momentous Christmas Day that, it can be fairly said, changed the history of the world. According to the contemporary biographer, Einhard, Charles was so surprised and annoyed by the Pope's action that he declared he would not have entered the church if he had known of Leo's intention. This statement seems to contradict all that we know about the preparations Charles made for assuming the imperial title. If he had not been expecting a momentous gift from the people of Rome and the Pope, why had he brought with him thousands of pounds of silver and gold to show his gratitude? If he was vexed with the Pope, why did he bring Leo's accusers to trial only a few days later

A sixteenth-century drawing preserves now-vanished portraits of Leo III (left) and Charles, which originally appeared in a mosaic made about 800 for a Roman church Leo had restored. In his arms the Pope holds a model of that church, which is his holy offering to God.

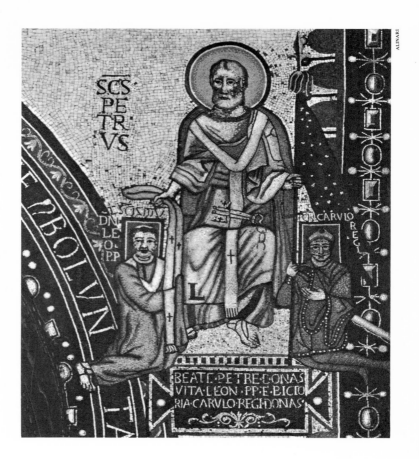

SCS PETRVS

BEATE·PETRE·DONAS VITA·LEON·PP·E·BICTO RIA·CARVLO·REGI·DONAS

A detail of the heavily restored mosaics in Rome's church of St. John Lateran shows St. Peter giving the pallium, an ecclesiastical vestment, to Pope Leo (left) and the standard of secular power to Charles. The mosaic was completed just before the coronation in 800.

and sentence them to death—a sentence commuted to banishment only at the intercession of Leo himself?

There have been many theories to explain Einhard's strange statement. Perhaps, it has been argued, Charles desired the imperial title but did not wish to be crowned by the Pope. But this theory arises out of awareness of conflicts between the popes and emperors only in the later Middle Ages. Moreover, Charles, immediately after his own coronation, permitted the Pope to crown his favorite son and heir, young Charles, as King of Frankland. As Charlemagne saw it, in performing a coronation, the Pope could not possibly be asserting the superiority of Church over State. The Pope was merely solemnizing what had already been won by arms. In fact, only a few days before, Charles had shown Rome his view of the relationship between the two powers ("the two swords," as medieval writers phrased it) by sitting in judgment on the Pope.

Another theory holds that Charles blamed Leo for anticipating events and crowning him prematurely; that he

A page from Einhard's biography of Charles documents the Frankish war against the Danes. "He dominated and submitted to tribute the barbaric and savage people," Einhard boasted of the outcome.

desired the imperial crown, had planned to take it, but wished to wait for the consent of the one authority he regarded as legitimately entitled to confer that crown: the Emperor at Constantinople. It is certainly true that in the years following his acclamation as Emperor in the West, Charles made repeated diplomatic efforts to win the approval of the Byzantine Emperor. He virtually sued for recognition and made considerable concessions of territory in order to obtain acknowledgment from the ruler at Constantinople as "brother emperor." However, at the time of his coronation, Charles regarded the imperial throne as vacant. In addition, he could scarcely expect the Emperor to confer a crown on him voluntarily. Charles had to wear it first; then he could bargain about his right to it.

It has also been suggested that Einhard may have been merely attempting to depict Charlemagne as modest—a show of reluctance to assume power even then was considered good form. Or the biographer could have been reporting some much later outburst on the part of Charles, some momentary anger with the burdens of his office or with Pope Leo personally. There is also the possibility that Einhard's memory was playing him false. He wrote his biography a quarter of a century or more after the coronation, so that he may well have unwittingly exaggerated or distorted some casual remark by Charles. Einhard in any case liked to think of his master as a Frankish king, closely identified with the Frankish people rather than with the varied nations of the Roman Empire. Thus the biographer's own bias may have influenced his memory of events.

Whatever his true feelings about the coronation, Charles certainly began at once to act like an emperor. He sent his *missi* through the papal territories to collect taxes and to gather from vassals new oaths of allegiance to Emperor Charles. He instituted a thorough shake-up of the corrupt administration in Rome and the other papal cities of Italy. He had new coins struck bearing the words "Restoration of the Empire." And for a time he even entertained the fantastic notion of marrying the cruel Empress Irene, thus reuniting the two parts of the Roman Empire. The plan could not possibly have succeeded, for the Empire was sundered irrevocably by the Moslem conquest of much of the Mediterranean world. But the project itself shows that

The ninth-century statue opposite, from the church of St. John in Münster, Switzerland, founded by Charles, is said to be a likeness of the Emperor.

119

A shroud of delicate Byzantine silk was discovered in Charles' tomb when it was opened in 1000. Still intact after another nine centuries, the detail of the fabric above reveals the topical motif: medallions of stylized elephants surrounded by sinuous flowers. At right, the ivory chess piece given Charles by Harun perhaps also commemorates the gift of Abul Abbas.

far from disdaining imperial grandeur, Charles dreamed of power and magnificence that would vie with that of Augustus Caesar eight hundred years earlier.

Before anything could come of the contemplated marriage, however, Irene was overthrown in a palace revolution in 802 and exiled to the island of Lesbos, where she soon died. Charles then began courting the new Emperor, Nicephorus, offering peace on the borders in return for recognition as Emperor. He had already been exchanging embassies with Harun al-Rashid, the powerful ruler of Islam, who was constantly warring with the Byzantine emperors. Negotiations with Harun were thus a means of applying pressure upon the Byzantine Empire. Little of political substance came of this flirtation, but the exchange of courtesies brought to Charles a number of gifts that excited admiration and awe in Frankland. A wonder of wonders was the elephant, Abul Abbas, an animal that no Frank of the day had ever seen. He became a great favorite with court and populace alike, and Charles took him along wherever he went, for the people to see. Unfortunately, the elephant died suddenly in 810. But by then other "Arabian Nights" gifts had arrived from "Aaron," as the Frankish annals called Harun al-Rashid: a magnificent silken tent, candelabra, and a mechnical clock with twelve

windows from which knights in armor came marching each hour when the clock struck.

These negotiations with the pagans did not mean that Charles, after winning the imperial crown, had become more tolerant of other religions or less earnest about his own. On the contrary, he made efforts to keep on good terms with Harun at least partly in order to protect the rights of Christian pilgrims to visit the Holy Land, whose churches he supported by lavish donations. In return for this support, he was rewarded with a gift, from the Patriarch of the Holy City, of keys to the Holy Sepulcher and to Jerusalem itself. And at home he continued, on an even greater scale, his efforts to correct abuses in Church and State. During the years after the coronation a stream of decrees poured from Charlemagne's chancery. He endeavored to enforce justice; to protect the poor, the widows, and the orphans; to compel the clergy to be an example of love, mercy, and charity to the people. Sometimes these decrees of his later years sounded more like sermons than state papers. Charles took on the tone of a Biblical prophet as he exhorted his subjects to be "not quarrelsome, not wrathful, not proud, not drunken; but chaste in heart and body, humble, modest, sober, merciful, peaceful."

At this time Charles also made efforts to ease the burdens of military service. He exempted the poorer freemen from army duty and gave permission for six or more smallholders to join together so that only one went to battle while the others provided his equipment and money for his support. Such relaxation of the stringent rules for military service was now possible because Charles' realm was largely at peace, although there was still constant skirmishing in the marches along the frontiers. But that was what those buffer zones had been created for: to keep war away from the heart of the empire.

In only one place within the empire did Charles find it necessary to fight again, and in person. After thirty years of almost unremitting warfare the Saxons had not yet been permanently subdued. In the region of swamps between the Weser and the Elbe rivers, where so many revolts had begun, the Saxons again began to ambush Frankish detachments and to assassinate imperial envoys and priests. The Saxons, as a Frankish chronicler once wrote angrily of their recurring revolts, "returned to paganism like a dog that returns to its vomit."

Charles, already in his sixties and rather stout, nevertheless led an army into Saxony, while he ordered his Slavic

The representation of celestial Jerusalem at left, from a book of the Gospels produced at Charles' court early in the ninth century, is a skillful Carolingian copy of an antique painting style. The stage-set city is fronted by four columns, above which is a frieze depicting the symbols of the four Evangelists and a scene showing the adoration of the Lamb of God.

allies to attack the Saxons from the east. As always, the Saxons could not resist the massed might of the Franks and their allies in open battle. The campaign was soon over, but this time Charles did not order execution of the Saxon rebels. Instead, he uprooted them forcibly from their homes and scattered them in small groups through Gaul and Germany. Thousands upon thousands of Saxon men, women, and children were taken from the land of their birth. One whole province of Saxony was given to the Slavs as a reward for their help. This harsh measure finally settled the problem. There simply were not enough Saxons left in any one place to venture another rebellion. Saxony had been pacified and Christianized after thirty-two years—but at untold cost in human suffering.

VII

LEGACY AND LEGEND

Early in the year 806 Charles brought all three of his sons to Aachen and convoked a national assembly. The time had come, he felt, to settle the succession and prevent any quarreling among his heirs after his death. In February, 806, he published a testament that settled the division of the realm. All the nobles present took oaths to support the conditions set forth in this testament, and a copy was given to Einhard for delivery to Pope Leo for witnessing and approval.

The Division of the Realm of 806 did little more than ratify existing conditions. In keeping with Frankish tradition, Charles had long ago conferred separate kingdoms on each of his three sons. Although he probably now regretted that earlier decision, there was no way he could undo it. Each of the sons had already reigned so long in his own subkingdom that there would surely be rebellion and fraternal warfare if Charles now attempted to cancel his previous arrangements.

In these circumstances, he did the best he could. He tried to keep each subkingdom a geographic entity. Louis received all of Aquitaine, Gascony, the Spanish March, southern Burgundy, Provence, and Septimania. Pepin was granted Italy and Bavaria and Alamannia south of the Danube. Young Charles had for his portion all the rest: northern Burgundy, northern Alamannia, Austrasia, Neustria, Thuringia, Saxony, and Frisia. Charles and Louis were both granted a road to Italy through the Alps, so that they could come to the aid of their brother if necessary, and Pepin likewise had a road north through the Duchy of Chur, in what is now Switzerland.

Often identified as Charlemagne, the ninth-century equestrian statue of a king opposite wears such Frankish attire as hose, tunic, and long riding cloak. Above, two fish form the initial letter "Q" in an early manuscript.

Throughout the text of this political testament Charles repeatedly reminded the brothers that they must live at peace with each other, never invade each other's territory, and always be ready to help each other against enemies. Each must permit his subjects to marry across the borders and to hold land in his brothers' kingdoms, in order to preserve some measure of unity. The three brothers also were commanded to continue the policy of protecting the Church as their father, grandfather, and great-grandfather before them had done. But nothing whatsoever was said about inheritance of the imperial title. Perhaps Charles meant to make his eldest son and namesake emperor and to arrange for the younger brothers to be subject to him. But if that was his plan, fate ruled otherwise.

Toward the end of the first decade of the new century, plague—the recurrent scourge of Europe and Asia—had begun to sweep through Italy and Central Europe. At the same time, the Vikings began to attack the fringes of Charlemagne's empire. Expecting an invasion by Göttrik, King of the Danes, Charles in 810 led an army to Verden, on the Aller River, where he had once massacred the forty-five hundred Saxons. The "curse" of Verden still held, for word was brought to him there that his favorite daughter,

A carved wooden standard from a ninth-century Viking ship—like those used for raids on Charlemagne's realm in the last years of his reign—ends in the snarling animal head at left. The vibrant relic is from a royal burial mound unearthed in Norway in 1904.

The engraved copper cover of a volume produced about 1100 commemorates the roles of Charles and Pepin the Short (top) as patrons of the Abbey of Prüm. Below Christ (center) are descendant kings.

Two more scenes from the St. Gall Psalter illustrate stages of medieval siege warfare. Above, cavalry and infantry surround a towered city, whose defenders peer out from behind stout walls. Opposite, a sad handful of survivors parleys with the attacking force across a corpse-littered field. Made in Switzerland between 872 and 920, the manuscript provides accurate depictions of such Carolingian weapons and armor as bows, lances, shields, helmets, and mail.

Rotrud, had died, probably of plague. Only a few months before, he had lost his sister, Gisla.

Blow upon blow followed. Still at Verden, Charles heard the terrible news that his son Pepin, King of Italy, had also died. Nor were men and women alone the victims of disease. The oxen used for transport and the cattle used for meat also were succumbing to a mysterious epidemic that rapidly spread through all Europe. Even Abul Abbas, the elephant, died. The people became so hysterical over the loss of their cattle that they believed foreign agents were poisoning the wells. Innocent persons were seized by frenzied mobs, charged with scattering poisonous powder, and thrown into rivers.

It was a time of tribulation. It must have been hard for Charles and his contemporaries not to believe that Verden was indeed accursed, for before he left the town, Charles himself was injured. The war against the Danes had come to nothing, because King Göttrik was assassinated and the Danes fell to squabbling among themselves; the attack against the Frankish kingdom never materialized. As Charles started the march back to Aachen, a meteor flashed across the pre-dawn sky. The Emperor's horse shied, and he was thrown to the ground so violently that he lost his

BOTH: STIFTSBIBLIOTHEK, ST. GALL; PHOTO ZUMBÜHL.

sword and his cloak. He was "disarmed and disrobed," wrote Einhard, who saw the fall as a portent.

Worse was to follow. The following year, 811, young Charles died at the beginning of December, leaving no heir. That seemed to mean that the Frankish realm would not be divided up but would be united under the old Emperor's sole surviving son, Louis. Although he had ruled Aquitaine for three decades—since he was three—Louis was, in fact, the most ineffectual of Charles' three direct heirs. His alleged preference for spiritual over temporal matters would in time bring him the name of Louis the Pious. The designation of Louis as Charlemagne's successor was not made without opposition. Pepin's son, Bernhard, was named to succeed his father as King of Italy, and there was some talk at court of giving him young Charles' domain as well— even of letting Bernhard succeed Louis, who was to be disinherited. Charlemagne, however, picked Louis to hold his far-flung empire together, although this son was destined to preside instead over its dissolution. No one knew it at the time, but with the death of young Charles there had passed the last hope for preservation of a united Europe.

In his sorrow the Emperor turned more and more to religion for solace. He discussed matters of doctrine with his

bishops and archbishops and began preparing a correct text of the four Gospels. He lost interest in the affairs of government. In the public squares his heralds read aloud commands from the Emperor that sounded more like commandments:

Be humble and kind to one another. . . .

Envy, hatred, and violence keep men from the Kingdom of God. . . .

Remember that the Apostle says we must all appear before the Judgment Seat of Christ. . . .

Life is short and the hour of death uncertain; it is wise to be prepared. Remember that it is a fearful thing to fall into the hands of God. Confess your sins, show penitence, give alms, and the Lord will be merciful. . . .

To ensure his proper credit with the Ruler of the next world, Charlemagne in 811 gave a good part of his fortune to the Church. All his personal wealth—gold, jewelry, garments—was divided into three lots. The first two lots were subdivided into twenty-one parts, each to go to an archbishop of Charles' realm. The third lot the Emperor reserved for use during his lifetime. Upon his death, however, the remaining treasure was to be divided once more— this time into four parts. One was to go to the twenty-one archbishoprics; one was to be given in alms to the poor; one was to be distributed among the palace servants; and only the fourth part—one twelfth of Charles' original wealth— was to be bequeathed to his heirs.

All his life Charles had enjoyed the best of health, but now, in his seventies, he began to be troubled by gout and fevers. He left his proper work to his underlings and began to put off decisions whenever he could. It took the arrival of ambassadors from Constantinople in 812 to stir him out of this distracted state. For the Byzantines had at last decided to grant him the recognition he craved. In return for a treaty of peace in which the Franks relinquished claims to Venetia and Dalmatia, the eastern ambassadors addressed Charles by the title of emperor. Only then did Charles consent to transfer the title to his surviving son, Louis.

All through the summer of 813 Charles kept Louis with him in Aachen, teaching his son—who was now a man of thirty-five, long married and with sons of his own—not

A kneeling member of the Byzantine embassy that reached Charlemagne in 812 offers him a gift.

Superimposed on Louis the Pious' portrait at left, from a manuscript poem of the ninth century dedicated to him, are letters that can be read down or across—like a crossword puzzle. His name, Hludowig, appears on the halo.

An illustration from a ninth-century arithmetic treatise personifies four of the seven liberal arts— from left, Music, Arithmetic, Geometry, and Astronomy. A comparison of events in the Gospels of Matthew, Mark, and Luke appears at right in a page from a book prepared at the Abbey of Tours during the years Alcuin served there, 796 to 804. A rat, attracted by the vellum's nutritious qualities, may have taken a bite from the page.

only "how to reign and keep order in the realm," but also "how he ought to live." Charles felt that his own strength was fast fading, and he knew only too well this son's weakness of character. In the short time that was left to him he did his best to teach Louis the principles that had made him a great ruler. He would never know how completely he had failed.

In September Charles called a great national assembly, one of the most glittering in his entire reign. It was attended by almost everyone of note throughout the empire. Leaning on his son's arm, for he was by now almost crippled with gout, Charles proposed to his dukes and counts, bishops and abbots, that Louis be elected emperor. The assembly unanimously approved, and formal investiture was set for Sunday, September 11.

On that day Charles once more arrayed himself in the splendid imperial robes he had so seldom worn. From head to foot he gleamed with gold: a golden diadem upon his brow, his robe made of cloth of gold, his boots sparkling with gold and gems. Accompanied by his son, he went to the high altar of the great octagonal church he had built. On the altar rested a golden crown, as thirteen years before a similar crown had lain on the altar in St. Peter's Basilica. Charles and Louis knelt in prayer for a long time.

r endroit comence
la vie et li fait
du debonaire re
loeys fils klul
le grant qui fu
rois et empereur · Mais p
ce que il porta couronne · et
fist auains grans fais au
vinant de son pere nous con
uendra parler de · klui · iuf
ques en auant · plusieurs
fames ot li empereres · la ·
& elles engendra grant
lignec de fils et de filles ·
La premiere de ces fames
ot non hildegarde ·

oble dame fu z
nce de la lig
ne de sadig
ne · y · hours
matles coaut
enseuble a la premiere fois
Des quieus li uns comenca
pres ausi tot amour ome
a naistre · Li autres qui p
la uolempte de nre seignor
nasqui plains de vie z for
mez · baptises fu et par
non apple; loeys · En lan
de lincarnacion nre seig
neur ihucrist sept cens
z soixante zz et dis z huit ·

t pource que il
fu nez en aqui
taine · Li pes
li ottria des
lors le voiau
me se diex li donnoit vie z
volt que il en fust sires cla
mez · bien sauoit li emper
qui tant estoit sages que ri
roiaumes est ausi come le
corps dun home qui souuet
est huites et deboute de dui
ses maladies · et vost mor
uoit auame fois se il uedo
it secourus par le conseil de
filique · Et tout ausi est

Then Charles rose. He turned to face the colorfully clad throng and began a long speech that once again turned into a rambling sermon. A priest-king, he preached to his kneeling son on the duties of a ruler. Louis must love God and fear Him, protect the Church, be kind to his kin, honor the priests, love the common people, help widows and orphans and the poor, be just to all men. Louis promised that he would obey all his father's behests. Charles then placed the crown on his head. He embraced his son, now co-Emperor, and both men wept.

It was later considered significant that Charles did not ask the Pope or any of his bishops to officiate at this coronation—as if he were determined to set a new precedent. It has been said that Charles foresaw that the Church might claim the right to crown emperors and thus set itself up as superior to the rulers. But this interpretation probably reads too much into the omission. Charles himself, it is likely, simply assumed that no religious authority could possibly be higher than the divinely appointed Emperor who governed both State and Church.

The coronation of his son was Charles' last public act. Afterward he seemed to recover his normal good health for a short time. Einhard writes that, old as Charles was, he spent the entire month of October hunting. But the winter was a harsh one, and during the third week in January he suffered one of his recurrent fevers. He tried to doctor himself, as was his habit, by fasting. But the fever developed into pleurisy, and a week later, on January 28, 814, he died at the age of seventy-one. He was laid to rest in the church he himself had built at Aachen.

In the inscription on his tomb, Charlemagne's subjects recorded that "the great and orthodox Emperor" had "nobly increased the kingdom of the Franks." That was one of the most obvious accomplishments of his reign and the one that most impressed his contemporaries. It was also destined to be the most short-lived.

Louis succeeded to the throne unopposed, but he was unable to retain what his father had won. He could not control his own nobles and bribed them to support him by giving away the very source of his own power and wealth, the royal estates that his father and forefathers had owned

Two last acts of Charlemagne appear in a mid-fourteenth-century history of France: at left, the aged Emperor reveals his last testament; at right, he watches a bishop crown Louis the Pious, inaccurately depicted as a child.

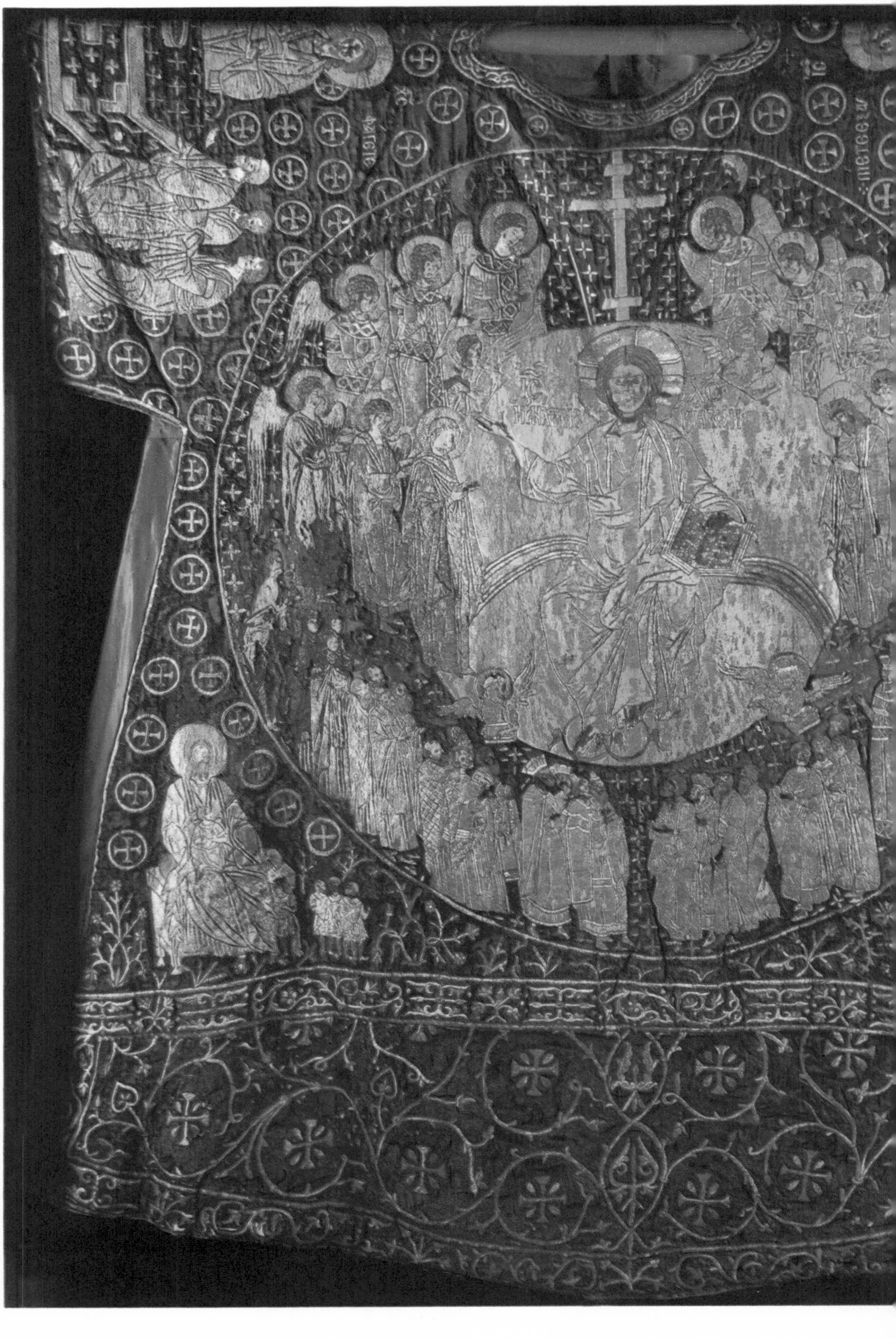

TRESOR DE L'ARCHEVECHE DE REIMS

IMPERIAL RELICS

Few objects exist that can, with any degree of certainty, be identified as actually having belonged to Charlemagne; indeed, some items are associated with the great medieval ruler only by tradition. The lavishly embroidered dalmatic at left, an ecclesiastical vestment for use at Mass, was once believed to have been worn by Charles at his coronation in 800—until it was discovered that it is of Byzantine origin and dates only to the fourteenth century. Undoubtedly Charlemagne's is the talisman above—it was found hanging around his neck when his tomb was opened in 1000. A work of embossed gold filigree, the amulet or charm is set with precious stones and was once supposed to hold hairs from the head of the Virgin Mary. Napoleon, falling heir to the ornament eight centuries later, substituted for the hairs a fragment of wood said to be from the True Cross and gave it to Josephine.

before his time. He also could not control his own sons, and when they had grown to manhood, they rebelled against him. They fought their father, and later they fought each other. By the time Louis the Pious died, twenty-six years after his father's death, the empire that Charlemagne had built was well on its way to disintegration.

In fairness, the breakup of the empire must not be attributed to Louis' personal weakness alone. He was not responsible for the Frankish tradition of dividing up the realm among sons as if an empire were the ruler's private property. Even Charlemagne had done this, although he recognized the dangers. To some extent the practice was justified by the conditions of the age. With communications so slow, it was difficult to govern a vast territory. The establishment of subkingdoms under an emperor whom the kings were bound to obey seemed a natural and sensible solution. But the plan foundered on the rocks of fraternal jealousies.

Louis was also only partly responsible for the rapid development of feudalism, which further undermined his rule by increasing the power of the territorial nobility and weakening the central government. Feudalism, it must be remembered, was basically a system of landholding that made society a pyramid. From the broad base of the peasantry to the king or emperor at the top, each man held land from someone above him, in return for certain services fixed rigidly by tradition or contract. Stated in this extremely simplified form, feudalism sounds like a system that would ease the task of governing for the man at the top of the pyramid. But in practice this was not at all the case. The great officers of state were repaid for their services to the crown by grants of "benefices" or "fiefs," vast estates and sometimes whole provinces from which they derived their revenues. Their earlships, dukedoms, constabularies, and so on tended to become hereditary. And when the king or emperor lost the power to dismiss them, he lost the power to make them obey him. Instead of his servants, they became his rivals.

The many wars of Charlemagne's reign had speeded the trend toward feudalization. Freemen unable to bear the burdens of military service "commended themselves" to some lord who had the resources to maintain a band of household knights. The freeman accepted a status of permanent dependency for himself and his descendants in return for protection and temporary relief from the demands of the central government. Sometimes, too, if a lord was

In a detail from the Charlemagne reliquary shown on page 89, Louis the Pious appears in high relief.

Like his father, Louis negotiated with Byzantine emperors. Here, the hand of God bestows a blessing as Louis receives ambassadors of Leo V, Eastern ruler during the early years of his long reign.

sufficiently powerful and unscrupulous, he would impose dependency by force upon the lesser men in his territory.

Charlemagne had been aware of the dangers and had used his *missi* to check the greed of the nobles. But Louis lacked his father's awesome personality; he feared his nobles—they did not fear him. Moreover, he foolishly destroyed the effectiveness of the one institution that served the interests of the central government alone. Instead of continuing to use the *missi* to restrain the territorial rulers, Louis yielded to the pressure of the lords and passed a decree stripping the *missi* of much of their power to interfere in local affairs.

The nobility did not thank him for this concession. In later years they repaid him by disloyalty. Twenty years after his father's death Louis found himself embroiled in a war with his sons that he had brought on himself. His army lay encamped near Colmar, facing the rebels across an open plain that forever after was to be called the Lügenfeld, the "Field of Lies." One night, after all efforts at mediation had failed, Louis' nobles and their followers began crossing

Two more panels from the roof of the chapel-shaped reliquary also shown on pages 84 and 89 depict scenes in Charlemagne's career. Below is the Emperor in his most customary role, that of a military commander. Surrounded by soldiers —some of whom appear to be dozing at left—Charles is outfitted with armor at the beginning of a battle. Opposite is the spiritual Charles. A priest absolves him of his sins (left) and then, standing at the altar, receives from a hovering angel a blessing for the Emperor, kneeling in prayer.

the field to the rebel camp. They deserted in such numbers that Louis was forced to give up the struggle. Humanely, he ordered the few who had remained faithful to him to cross the field also, so that they would not be killed in a hopeless fight against overwhelming numbers. Then he surrendered and for some time was held prisoner by his own sons.

Those sons, in their turn, had not only each other to contend with, but also the "fury of the Northmen." The weakened and divided empire could no longer hold the Vikings at bay. The long ships of the Northmen sailed far up the rivers of the empire, plundering churches and cities, ravaging monasteries, despoiling the rich farmlands of the river valleys. Only a navy could have opposed them, and there was no Frankish navy. Charlemagne had recognized the need for one and had begun building ships in his last years, but by then it was too late. "The Franks were landlubbers," a great historian has remarked—and landlubbers they remained in the reign of Charlemagne's grandsons and great-grandsons as well. The assaults of the Vikings accelerated the ruin of the Carolingian Empire.

THE VIKINGS

The short, sudden raids of the Northmen against settlements on the fringes of Charlemagne's empire soon turned into prolonged invasions that terrorized the entire Continent. In the century following the great ruler's death, Vikings nearly conquered the British Isles, established a kingdom in Russia, stood at the walls of Constantinople, and reached Iceland—en route eventually to America. The intrepid adventurers followed this route of discovery and conquest in long-prowed ships like those shown in the twelfth-century illustration opposite of Danes arriving in England. At right are three artifacts of the Viking era: Carved from bone, the Swedish Viking at top wears a conical helmet that continues into a slim, pointed nose shield. The imaginatively carved horse-head at bottom was found in 1880 in a burial ship. The mounted Viking below, an ivory chessman, is from Scotland's western isles.

A. T. A., STOCKHOLM

NATIONAL MUSEUM OF ANTIQUITIES OF SCOTLAND

UNIVERSITETETS OLDSAKSAMLING, OSLO

Although the empire splintered after his death, Charlemagne's other achievements were more lasting. One of the greatest of these was the colonization of Europe. "Colonization" seems a strange word, but that is what it was: the establishment of colonies in hitherto empty lands. Europe in the eighth and ninth centuries was a thinly populated continent of vast forests, here and there broken by settlements. Even in districts of ancient civilization, much land had fallen out of cultivation, gone back to brush and forest after the collapse of the Roman Empire. Charlemagne vigorously promoted the resettlement of the land, and that peaceful reconquest of Europe continued after his death, though interrupted at times by Viking raids.

Another of the lasting effects of Charlemagne's reign was the growth of towns and trade. The new roads he had built, the inns he had established for pilgrims and merchants, and the general safety and security of life within the confines of the empire naturally aided peaceful trade. The increase of wealth resulting from revived commercial life stimulated the arts and crafts, as did the Emperor's activities as a builder. The wider horizons of a vast empire, which on its borders was in contact with the Byzantine and Islamic cultures, brought a new sophistication to the life of central Europe. Painters, sculptors, ivory carvers, goldsmiths, and other artists and artisans found their way from Rome, Constantinople, and even Baghdad to the cities of France and Germany. The result was a cross-fertilization of ideas and skills that is so vitally important to development in the arts.

It was above all as the patron of learning that Charlemagne's influence continued after his death. His son and grandsons on the throne continued to draw scholars, poets, and philosophers to their courts. The schools in the great monasteries that Charlemagne had fostered and endowed, such as Fulda, Tours, St. Gall, Lorsch, and Reichenau, preserved the tradition of searching inquiry and love of books that had radiated from Charlemagne's Palace Academy. The term "Carolingian Renaissance" has been applied to the age; but it must be acknowledged as something of an exaggeration if it implies the great flowering of the human spirit that characterized the fifteenth and sixteenth centuries. Yet by comparison with the state of art, science, literature, and philosophy before Charlemagne's day, what took place under his rule and that of his successors was a true Revival of Learning. For centuries to come, the fame of Frankish scholars spread. When King Alfred of England

A scene of heavenly exaltation appears in this page from the Utrecht Psalter, produced near Reims about 832. An angelic host, looking strangely like Carolingian peasants, heralds the arrival of Christ as four men at bottom center struggle mightily to pump air into an ancient organ. In his youth, Charles had seen Frankland's first organ—a Byzantine gift to King Pepin.

became concerned about the woeful state of education in his country, he sent to Frankland for teachers. It has been said that Charlemagne, with the help of Alcuin, laid the basis for all modern education. This, too, is something of an exaggeration. But the schools fostered by Charlemagne did ultimately develop into the great universities of Europe and thus were the ancestors of our own institutions of higher learning.

Perhaps even more impressive than all of Charlemagne's success in changing the physical and intellectual life of Europe was the force that his personality exerted upon the medieval imagination. That enduring spell was assured by the biography that his architect-friend Einhard wrote of him, a biography cast in the classical spirit and language of the Roman historian Suetonius. It was further nourished by a rather fanciful book called *The Feats of Charlemagne*, written by a monk of St. Gall some seventy years after the Emperor's death. The monk's Charlemagne is larger than life, supreme in all the attributes of a ruler, a man of iron, but at the same time all-wise, all-merciful.

Thereafter there was no stopping the growth of legend. A vast cycle of poetic romances began, in which almost every trace of the historical Charlemagne was obliterated. *The Song of Roland* was only the greatest example of those innumerable tales in which Emperor Charlemagne became the embodiment of all the ideals of the Middle Ages: the greatest of crusaders against the Saracens, the justest of judges, the most gallant of knights, the most generous of lords. What King Arthur was to Britain, Charlemagne became to France.

But alongside this mythical Charlemagne there always remained some memory of the historical personality. That memory was especially cherished by the kings and emperors who came after him and who strove repeatedly to create once more his unified Christian realm, an empire in which Church and State would work together in harmony. The "golden age of Charlemagne," as medieval men thought of it, could not be revived. But his empire remained a hope and a goal throughout the Middle Ages; and the force of his vision is not spent even today. The only "united Europe" that could conceivably arise in the twentieth century would be, geographically, a reconstitution of the empire of Charlemagne.

A ninth-century manuscript made at Tours contains what has been identified as the oldest surviving illustration of an actual contemporary event (left). The scene is a ceremony, about 846, in which an illuminated Bible was presented to an enthroned Charles the Bald (center), Louis' son and successor. This view, along with a dedicatory poem, appeared in the gift volume.

Royal book bindings were sometimes as lavish as the one opposite that adorns the Golden Book of St. Emmeram, made about 870 at Reims or St. Denis. The central figure of Christ is flanked by the four Evangelists, with four panels illustrating Gospel stories above and below. Precious stones set in gold filigree stud the margins.

147

FURTHER READING

Bullough, Donald A., *The Age of Charlemagne.* Putnam, 1965.

Easton, Stewart C., and Wieruszowski, Helene, *The Era of Charlemagne.* Van Nostrand, 1961 (paperback).

Fichtenau, Heinrich, *The Carolingian Empire*, translated by Peter Munz. Blackwell, 1957.*

Lamb, Harold, *Charlemagne: The Legend and the Man.* Doubleday, 1954.

Munz, Peter, *The Origin of the Carolingian Empire.* Humanities Press, 1960 (paperback).

Pirenne, Henri, *Mohammed and Charlemagne.* Barnes & Noble, 1955.*

Sullivan, Richard E., *Aix-la-Chapelle in the Age of Charlemagne.* The University of Oklahoma Press, 1963.

Sullivan, Richard E., ed., *The Coronation of Charlemagne.* Heath, 1959 (paperback).

Wallace-Hadrill, John M., *The Barbarian West*, A.D. 400-1000. Hillary House, 1952.*

Wallace-Hadrill, John M., *The Long-Haired Kings and Other Studies in Frankish History.* Barnes & Noble, 1962.

Winston, Richard, *Charlemagne, from the Hammer to the Cross.* Bobbs-Merrill, 1954.*

*Also available in paperback.

Blowing a horn at right, Roland rallies his troops under the walls of Pampeluna in a fourteenth-century Italian miniature.

HORIZON CARAVEL BOOKS

JOSEPH L. GARDNER, *Editor*

Janet Czarnetzki, *Art Director*

Sandra L. Russell, *Copy Editor*

Laurie P. Phillips, *Picture Editor*

Kathleen Fitzpatrick, *Assistant Copy Editor*

Annette Jarman, *Editorial Assistant*

Gertrudis Feliu, *Chief, European Bureau*

ACKNOWLEDGMENTS

The editors are particularly grateful for the valuable assistance of Miss Bianca Spantigati in Rome and Mrs. Maria Todorow in Florence. In addition, they would like to thank the following:

Archivio Capitolare, Modena
Bayerische Staatsbibliothek, Munich
Biblioteca Capitolare, Modena
Biblioteca Marciana, Venice
Bibliotheque Nationale, Paris—Marcel Thomas, Mrs. Le Monnier, Mrs. Caucheteux
Convent of San Paolo Fuori le Mura, Rome
Museo dell'Opera del Duomo, Monza— Giovanni Rigàmonti
Österreichische Nationalbibliothek, Vienna—Dr. Hans Pauer
Royal Library, Brussels—Martin Wittek
Staatsbibliothek, Bamberg
Staatsbibliothek, Bremen
Staatsbibliothek Stiftung Preussischer Kulturbesitz, Berlin—Dr. Roland Klemig
Staatliche Museen, Berlin—Dr. Arno Schönberger
Stadtbibliothek, Trier

BIBLIOTECA MARCIANA, VENICE: COD. FR. XXI, COLL. 257 FOL 107 V

149

Leafy vines encircle letters spelling "Te Igitur," the first Latin words of the Mass Canon—a service represented by the priest at center. The initials are from an 850 book made for the Bishop of Metz.

INDEX

Boldface indicates pages on which maps or illustrations appear